ELIZABETH R. SKOGLUND

DIVINE RECYCLING

LIVING ABOVE YOUR CIRCUMSTANCES

Divine Recycling
© 2010 by Elizabeth R. Skoglund.
All rights reserved.

This book was originally published as *Making Bad Times Good*,
© 1991 by Triumph Books, an imprint of Gleneida Publishing
Group, Tarrytown, New York. This book is updated and includes
additional new material.

Unless otherwise noted, scriptural citations are taken from the King
James Version.

Verses marked TLB are taken from *The Living Bible*, © 1971 by
Tyndale House Publishers, Wheaton, IL. Used by permission.

All material by Ruth Bell Graham used by permission.

Cover design by John Whorrall Sr. and John Whorrall Jr.

The patients mentioned in this book are real, and their stories are
true. However, to protect their privacy, names and other identifying
details have been changed.

ISBN   978-0-615-27705-9

LCCN 2009937439

Printed in the United States of America.

CONTENTS

To Matthew and Lucie Pearl Conolly

PREFACE

A number of years ago I told a student who was interning in my counseling office about my intentions to write a book about what works in counseling. It would include something of the integration that is possible between biblical Christianity and sound psychological principles. I told him I would have to be older and more experienced first. I would have to be ready.

Years later that former student called me on the telephone and asked, "Do you think you're ready to write that book yet?" His question came as a bit of a jolt. I didn't feel that much older. I thought about his question and decided that after eighteen years of private practice, added onto six years of counseling high school students, perhaps I was ready.

Making Bad Times Good was the result of that call. Now, once again a number of years later I have updated that book and in so doing have not only added greater knowledge and experience from my years as a psychotherapist but I have included some valuable help in areas like brain plasticity and insight into some of the spiritually questionable areas like the Emergent Church and its affect on the counseling process.

Divine Recycling deals with a method of psychotherapy which I have called Dimension Therapy, a therapy which not only integrates body, mind, and spirit in its treatment but does it on various levels for each of those areas, depending on individual needs.

Divine Recycling distills what has worked for people I have counseled on a variety of problems – children, as well as adults of all ages, men as well as women. The solutions to problems are at the same time simple and profound. They can be applied within limits or with a completeness that can be life transforming. Their success in improving any individual's life depends, at least in part, on that person's willingness to change and to resolve never to stop growing.

Every once in a while a small child asks permission to move into my office. However, a counseling office is never a place in which to live. It is a place to go out from. It is a place of comfort and equipping.

If it is sound, psychological counseling should not be shunned by Christians, and Christianity should not be denigrated by those who offer psychological help. People are made up of body, mind, and spirit, and what helps one part of a person usually helps the whole person.

Ultimately, when we humans have done all that we can do to heal the mind or the body or the spirit, it is still God who effects the cure. Yet more often than not, God uses mortals in the process of curing. That part is what *Divine Recycling* is all about.

ACKNOWLEDGMENTS

Starting with Rob Jones who originally urged me to write on this topic, many people have inspired, supported, and actually contributed to the finished product.

When I first changed from educator to psychotherapist, a psychologist, Glenn K. Wiest, and two psychiatrists, Harvey Ross, M.D., and G.L. Harrington, M.D., were my mentors. They are all gone now but not forgotten. Writers like Rollo May, Viktor Frankl, William Glasser, Amy Carmichael, Paul Tournier, and C.S. Lewis, with the exception of Frankl and Glasser, were people I never met but were deeply influential in my development of a multi-dimensional form of therapy. A teacher from high school, Beverly West, and a principal/teacher, Pamela Reeve, herself a writer and counselor, were each a major influence throughout my life as were my parents, Betty and Ragnar Skoglund, who thought no goal was too high to attempt, no failure too great to overcome.

My thanks go to Lance and Rayne Wilcox and Elizabeth Hannah Wilcox for hours on the computer, countless practical tasks, emotional support, and much prayer. Along with others like Matthew and Lucie Pearl Conolly, Ken and Carolyn Connolly, Rachel and Andrew Chu, John and Lynn Whorrall, Karl Weiskopf, and Richard Baltzell, they also contributed greatly by sorting out ideas, reading chapters and praying. Netmenders, a small women's group which meets in my home, offered much valued, consistent prayer support.

Once again I am uniquely grateful to the late Ruth Bell Graham for taking time to be interviewed and to Evelyn Freeland for aiding in the details of those interviews. Ultimately, I will always treasure the notes, books, and other evidences of personal support which Ruth gave me.

My thanks, also, to those not mentioned here who encouraged and prayed. Any book involves a host of people encountered in the process of its inception and completion who then go their way but are nevertheless important to the finishing of that book.

In the words of Amy Carmichael:

> Take this book in Thy wounded Hand,
> Jesus, Lord of Calvary,
> Let it go forth at Thy command,
> Use it as it pleaseth Thee.
>
> Dust of earth, but Thy dust, Lord,
> Blade of grass in Thy Hand a sword,
> Nothing, nothing unless it be
> Purged and quickened, O Lord, by Thee.

FOREWORD

With a skillful blend of clinical insight, Bible principles, and lucid illustrations, author/therapist Elizabeth Skoglund brings helpful counsel for readers of all ages. This blending of material powerfully leads to potential recovery, wholeness, and growth.

Much-needed discussion is presented on questions regarding the utilization of psychotherapy in meeting human needs. This book, rather than denying clinical therapy and medication in treatments, seeks to sensibly integrate all workable elements. Comprehensive counseling tools are seen as God-given tools for healing.

Equally strategic are the insights into the Emergent Church concepts in current practice. In this text we find undeniable devotion to the Word of God, professional experience, and passion for leading people of all ages to healthy balance of spirit, mind, and body.

Divine Recycling: Living Above Your Circumstances holds wisdom for family members, pastors, church and business leaders, lay counselors, missionaries, and adults and young people of all ages.

– John M. Whorrall, former Pastor Emeritus,
University Bible Church in Los Angeles, California

Remembering John M. Whorrall

Friend and Long-time Pastor of University Bible Church in Los Angeles, California

Within one month of his summons to his heavenly Home, John made his final earthly contributions to this work, a work which focuses on integrating biblical principles with sound psychotherapy. He emailed his comments on the Forward for *Divine Recycling* and then, within days of his leaving us, and without even being asked, he designed the cover, along with some collaboration with his son, John Whorrall Jr.

For a forthcoming book, *Finishing Well*, which is based on the lives of some Godly giants of the past, like David Livingstone and Francis Ridley Havergal, John sent a CD of his drawings of each of them so that these images could be used in the book.

John never stopped doing God's work. He never really retired. Whether it was those one-to-one lunches with someone who needed encouragement or advice or teaching a Bible study to a group of people whom others may have forgotten, John went on and finished well. Many of us may not have thought that his task here was done, but in the words of Charles H. Spurgeon, a nineteenth-century pastor whom John deeply respected: "You are immortal till your work is done."

To me, a stanza from "Rugby Chapel," written about his own father by nineteenth-century poet Matthew Arnold, sums up the life of John Whorrall:

If, in the paths of the world,
Stones might have wounded thy feet,
Toil or dejection have tried
Thy spirit, of that we saw
Nothing – to us thou wast still
Cheerful, and helpful, and firm!
Therefore to thee it was given
Many to save with thyself:
And, at the end of thy day,
O faithful shepherd! to come,
Bringing thy sheep in thy hand.

INTRODUCTION

Drop Thy still dews of quietness,
'Til all our strivings cease,
And let our ordered lives confess
The beauty of Thy peace.

Those of us reared in the days when hymns often contained two
or more thoughts in one line, and single phrases were not repeated
up to sixteen times as an unholy mantra, may treasure words like
these. But what do they really mean? What are the "still dews of
quietness?" How can our chaotic lives become "ordered?" What is
the nature of the "beauty of God's peace?"

These are difficult questions, and there is no one answer that
can satisfy all of them. For sure, St. Paul tells us to be "fearful for
nothing," but to rely on "prayer, petitions and thanksgiving," so
that "the peace of God, which passeth all understanding shall keep
(guard) your hearts and minds through Christ Jesus."

However, the God who made mankind has created a wonderfully
complex, psychological, neurochemical organism, and has set
mankind in an almost equally complex environment which may
impinge on our consciousness and attitudes in innumerable
ways; for we are the product of our genes, our upbringing, our
environment, our allergies, and other disorders of health.

Ms. Skoglund has attempted, no, succeeded in placing before us
a detailed description of this complexity in *Divine Recycling*. She
offers a shrewdly balanced analysis of the complexities of this life.
We are not psychological jellyfish borne wherever the currents of
life would carry us. She challenges those who all too readily cower

behind negative thoughts and self-images (no matter where they come from, no matter who originated them) to shut off the negative thought patterns which may have consumed their lives, to "cut and refocus" on more positive thoughts. Her balanced view, however, looks beyond those who need to "cut and refocus" to those who have depression caused by biochemical disorders of the brain. In, for this reviewer, the most interesting aspect of this book, she explores the still very new discoveries which link potentiation of serotonin effects in the brain with amelioration of depression. She considers the role of dopamine-dependent mechanisms in pleasure, rewards, and addictions of various kinds (drugs, gambling, and even shopping!). More boldly yet, she has examined the interplay between the amygdala and the hippocampus. She looks at the still very recent findings which suggest that defects of the amygdala might underlie various forms of antisocial behavior.

Just as the voice of a descant soprano will at times rise above the other voices of the choir like a stream of liquid silver, throughout this book Ms. Skoglund's firm belief that a loving God rules over it all emerges again and again. If we are perplexed by our neurochemistry, God is not. Step by step He leads researchers to new discoveries which, as no less a luminary than Freud himself suggested, may one day be seen as the "dews of quietness." With the aid of such God-given remedies, perhaps even the most troubled minds may truly appreciate the "beauty of God's peace." Then truly will Divine Recycling have occurred!

– Matthew E. Conolly, M.D.
Professor, David Geffen School of Medicine at UCLA

Epigraph

THE other day, it was the Lord's Day morning, two sparrows fell from the leads of my church into the vestry, which has a lofty glass skylight. As soon as they had recovered from their astonishment at finding themselves prisoners, they flew up against this skylight as though to break through it to the open heaven, and then round and round the room. They were desperately afraid of myself and the verger, whom I had called, not realizing that we were as anxious as they to get them out again into the air. The only thing we could do to help them was to keep them from alighting to rest; so with long brooms and soft missiles we constantly drove them from every cornice and pictureframe on which they alighted, till they fell exhausted, and with panting breasts, to the ground. Then we captured them and set them free. They might have said many a time, in the course of that encounter, "We were at ease, and they brake us asunder; they also set us up for their mark." But if they could review that episode now, they would doubtless see that it was love which forbade them to rest anywhere in the vestry, because it desired to give them their fullest liberty.

So with Job. God would not allow him to rest in anything short of the best, and therefore He broke up his nest. Is not this the key to his dealings with you? Oh, believe that behind the perpetual change and displacement of your life God is leading you into the glorious liberty of his children!

– F. B. Meyer

I knew the mass of men concealed
Their thoughts, for fear that if revealed
They would by other men be met
With blank indifference, or with blame reproved;
I knew they lived and moved
Tricked in disguises, alien to the rest
Of men, and alien to themselves – and yet
The same heart beats in every human breast!
… Ah! well for us, if even we,
Even for a moment, can get free
Our heart, and have our lips unchained;
For that which seals them hath been deep ordained!

– Matthew Arnold, The Buried Life

ONE

A SAFETY ZONE OF DISCOVERY

What rock do I lean on all week when you aren't there?" The question, thrown out as a parting statement, left me a little stunned with its directness. Mary had just finished her first counseling session with me. She impressed me as being a very intelligent lady, even though she wouldn't have agreed. In truth, Mary had a very low opinion of herself, an opinion reflected in her lack of care in dressing and in the flow of demeaning remarks she made about herself. "People don't like me, and I don't blame them" was a good example of her low self-esteem.

I was the third in a series of counselors to whom she had turned in her struggle with depression. In her sessions with the first counselor, she had found great comfort in her otherwise isolated existence, but no concrete long-range help. The second counselor had offered greater direction, but Mary had resisted the scariness of growth and change. With me she had found once again that sense of safety and encouragement that should be part of the counseling experience, but she was also once again confronted with the challenge to change. Paradoxically, until that change occurred, Mary would feel vulnerable. As a person who had few other safety zones in her life, when she left a counseling session she might feel that she was leaving her major safety zone. She might again want to ask, "What rock do I lean on when you aren't there?"

Anyone who seeks counseling is at that time in need of a safety zone. Safety zones are anchors. Safety zones help prevent burnout. They include special places, significant people, things, and even ideas that stabilize us in times of uncertainty, comfort us in times of difficulty, and equip us to go on and become whole. As a safety zone, counseling should be a place of comfort, protection, and encouragement, but it should be also a place of growth and change; and it must always be a place where people can develop tools that enable them to face life more effectively. It is a place where one can deal with negative mental recordings, like *what if* or *why not*. It is a place where one can learn to cut these negative messages and to declare boundaries. It is a place of refurbishing.

The safety zone of counseling is normally meant to be temporary; if it becomes a place of permanent residency, the positive benefits can turn into stunted growth and destruction. What is a legitimate crutch enabling healing becomes crippling in itself if it is used beyond its time of need. Then what once enabled growth and independence fosters a crippling dependence.

When I was in high school biology, we were asked to do a science project for extra credit. I chose to do one that involved hatching chicken eggs in an incubator. The school lent me an incubator, and I bought fertilized eggs from a nearby hatchery.

At the outset, all went well. For the first few hours and then days, I opened an egg, observed the developing chick under a microscope, and made drawings of what I saw. Then, as the embryos began to grow bigger, I just waited for the day when they would hatch.

By the time Easter vacation arrived, the chicks were overdue. My biology teacher suggested that I take the incubator home for the week. Day after day I waited. Nothing. After three or four days of vacation, I called a hatchery. Their conclusion was that the chicks had died in the shell. The only way to find out was to open one.

Armed with the moral support of a friend, I cautiously picked at one of the shells. No movement. I picked more. Still no movement. Then I saw that the shell contained a full-grown chick, but the chick was dead. Not wanting to take a chance on even one live chick being destroyed, I painstakingly opened each egg. Each one contained a small, dead chick, until I got to the last egg, which, for some reason

I don't remember, happened to be that of a duck. Inside there was a slight movement. I was there just in time to get it out before it too died. With a lot of care, the duck survived and became a pet.

When I finished opening the eggs, I was pretty shaken up. So I called the hatchery back to ask why the chicks had died, and I was told that they had died because of lack of moisture. The school incubator had not regulated this factor properly.

For a number of days the eggs had sheltered and nourished these chicks. The embryos had developed the circulatory systems that I had observed under the microscope. They had been fed by the nutrients in the egg yolk. They had developed little feet and beaks. They had grown to their full size. Then their little place of growth and safety became a death trap. They had stayed there too long.

Nature is full of such illustrations. A young plant that grows and is nurtured in a pot gradually becomes root bound and dies if it stays in that same small pot. The magnificent butterfly develops from the lowly caterpillar only as it breaks out of the chrysalis that has provided shelter but now would cause its death if it remained. The beautiful shell of the chambered nautilus is formed because the small sea creature grows a new chamber each time it outgrows the old. In each case the organism must leave the place that once provided comfort and life itself if it is to survive and grow.

In the same way the safety zone of counseling – as well as other safety zones, like friendship, a favorite restaurant, or a weekend retreat – is meant to be a place of refurbishment and renewal, a place to go out from and, at times, to return to. Even in our relationship with God, which is our only permanent safety zone, we still don't live in the building where we worship; we don't stay forever on our knees in prayer. We go out from that safety zone into the world, equipped and blessed from our encounter with God. A safety zone is not a comfort zone. It is not a place of self-pity or self-indulgence. It is a place of positive recovery and growth.

*   *   *

Christine, a child of eight, came with her father for his counseling sessions and read books in my waiting room. One day I invited her in alone for a few minutes. She cried while she told me how unhappy she was because her parents argued all the time. She was sure that they were headed for a divorce. After that I managed to get a few minutes alone with her each week, time stolen from her father's time and my break. She usually cried, and I tried to encourage her. I learned from her father that she eagerly anticipated each session, and so I was always careful to spend a little time with her. My office and my relationship became an important safety zone in her life, even with the limitations of time.

One evening after a couple of months had passed, Christine bounced into my office with a huge smile on her face. She flung her coat on a chair, spread out her arms dramatically, and exclaimed, "Boy, this counseling sure works!" I didn't need to ask why. In this instance only one thing would have made her this happy. Her parents weren't fighting anymore. Interestingly enough, the next week Christine chose to stay home and play with a friend rather than see me. For the time, and perhaps forever, Christine had outgrown counseling as her place of comfort and growth. She was going on.

To view counseling as a place incorporates some of the best philosophy that has been developed regarding the basic function of counseling. Psychiatrist Paul Tournier has so beautifully stated:

> The giving of a place to those who have none seems to me to be one way of defining our vocation as healers of persons…in helping our patients to find their places we are helping them to become persons. And that place is no abstraction. It is our consulting room, the

> fireside, the photographs on the mantelpiece,
> the clock they detest, the books on the shelves,
> all the little details with which they have become
> familiar during those hours that have been so
> important in their lives...how many patients
> find it hard to leave when the consultation is
> over, to leave this place![1]

If finding a place or, as I like to call it, a safety zone, provides a basis for emotional healing, then the kind of uprooting that we find in our life-styles in the twenty-first century is a cause for our feeling of lack of place. We buy services, move frequently, change jobs, dispose of friends, and then wonder why we have so few resources with which to face the ordinary demands of life, to say nothing of the extraordinary demands involved in just living in this age of high-tech medicine and nuclear threat.

For example, what other generation has had to decide when to turn off a respirator or whether to redefine death? Fifty years ago all a physician had to do was try to save lives; when people died, they simply stopped breathing. Yet at the same time what other generation has fought so hard for independence and then spent so many hours in counseling offices trying to get rid of the resultant feelings of isolation and loneliness? We long for closeness, but we fear its price tag.

In further describing this place, this safety zone called counseling, in what has been for me the best definition of counseling that I have ever heard, psychologist Rollo May remains unique in aptness of description. To him the age-old image of the hearth best conveys the intimacy and warmth of the counseling relationship:

> It is like inviting the traveler from his snowy
> and chilly journey to warm himself for an
> hour before the fire on another's hearth. Such
> understanding, it is not too much to say, is the

> most objective form of love. That is why there is
> always a tendency on the part of the counselee
> to feel some love toward the counselor, this
> person "who understands me." There are few
> gifts that one person can give another in this
> world as rich as understanding.[2]

Dr. Paul Tournier uses the same fireside image, but in a more literal way:

> When people come to see me in order to know
> and understand themselves better I interview
> them at my fireside.... For all of us the fire in
> the hearth is a powerful symbol, full of poetic
> meaning: it gives warmth, it is alive, it dies
> down and burns up again, it must be stirred, it
> is fascinating; it is a focus, a radiant center.[3]

The intimacy of the hearth brings the definition of *counseling* close to that of *friendship*, even though it goes without saying that it must also be an ideal and safe friendship with more than the usual structure, boundaries, and goals. Still, at its basis a good counseling relationship includes many of the same qualities as a good friendship. Sometimes counseling is merely a substitute for what could be accomplished in a close friendship.

In times of extreme stress human beings have survived only in strong supportive groups, in the safety zone of relationships. In the history of World War II, the Holocaust still offers some of the most striking examples of this. A study of survivors of Hitler's concentration camps states:

> Friendship was essential to survival, especially
> within the little groups which were constituted
> – groups of three or four people – our "families,"
> as we called them. There were a few people who

remained isolated, and they died. You simply couldn't survive alone.[4]

In a remarkable little book, *Dachau Sermons,* Lutheran pastor and concentration camp survivor Martin Niemöller described the meeting together of several inmates in the concentration camp where he himself was imprisoned. During several years of confinement in one of Hitler's camps, the meetings in Cell 34 amounted to only "six vacation hours!" Those who met were a Dutch cabinet minister, two Norwegian shippers, a British major, a Yugoslavian diplomat, and a Macedonian journalist. They were Calvinists, Lutherans, Anglicans, and Greek Orthodox. In a Communion service held on Maundy Thursday, March 29, 1945, Pastor Niemöller said to those who had gathered in Cell 34 in Dachau concentration camp:

> To this great community of those who proclaim the death of their Lord as a message of joy belong this evening also we, who come here to his table. A small company, everyone of us torn away from his earthly home and from the circle of his dear ones, all of us robbed of freedom and ever uncertain about what the following day or even the following hour will bring. But, despite all this, we are at home. We eat and drink at the table of our heavenly Father and we may be comforted. There is nothing that could tear us away and separate us from him, since our Lord and Master gave his life for us and for many, indeed, even for both of the friends who have gone away from our circle and whom we remember in our intercession, even for our dear ones far away or out there at the fronts, for whom we are anxious. For them also

did the Lord die, and with him they and we are
well protected.[5]

In the fellowship of God and in the company of a few of His
believers, this man who had been imprisoned in his own country
for standing against that country's evil could say, "We are at home."

At the same time in history, friendships that were of an intensity
and intimacy of trust common to a good counseling relationship
also provided a safety zone to those outside of the camps who were
part of the resistance movement. A Dutch woman, Miep Gies, was
largely responsible for hiding Anne Frank and her family in Holland.
As the war continued, just getting food for those she was hiding as
well as for her husband, Henk, and herself was a major task. They
did without and there was little time to focus on anything but
survival for themselves, the Frank family, and the others in hiding
with them.

Miep and Henk became friends with a Dutch couple who lived
across the street from them. Sometimes the four of them would sit
up late to drink a coffee substitute and listen, illegally, to the BBC.

One night Miep and Henk were feeling particularly discouraged.
On impulse, Miep took the last of the real coffee she had hidden
away, grabbed Henk's hand, and, after curfew, dashed across the
street to share it with their friends. Showing the result of not just
coffee but of the safety zone of closeness and trust that existed in
contrast to the hell around them, Miep recalled:

> Making each drop of rich coffee last as long as
> possible, we savored, in every way, the smell,
> taste, effect. It worked like magic. Soon, we
> were animated and again full of spit and vinegar
> against the German oppressor. Once again we
> were no longer beaten down, just biding our
> time until the Allies could get to us....We had
> made good use of our last real coffee.[6]

The safety zone of relationships had comforted them and then sent them out into the dark night of Hitler's war, refurbished and able to go on.

* * *

Even in so-called normal life, none of us lives unto ourselves. We still need the safety zone of relationships that feed us and nurture us. English pubs are an example of people getting together casually after a day's work, celebrating the small triumphs of each day, and commiserating together over the failures. Once a week, on Tuesday, C. S. Lewis, J. R. R. Tolkien, and Charles Williams met together at their favorite Oxford pub, the Eagle and Child. There they talked about their writing, speculated on ideas, and drank beer. Sometimes, too, the Inklings, as this group called itself, met in Lewis's rooms at Magdalen College at Oxford.

In referring to one such meeting of the Inklings, Lewis wrote of his conversion, "I have just passed on from believing in God to definitely believing in Christ – in Christianity. I will try to explain this another time. My long night talk with Dyson and Tolkien had a good deal to do with it."[7] Such is the potential of a safety zone.

In America many seek a bar after work because they cannot bear to leave the pressure of the workplace only to trade it for the pressure of the home – or the loneliness of the home in some cases. One suspects, however, that the focus is less on beer and more on hard liquor and that the ideas discussed do not normally attempt the height of those of the Oxford Inklings.

In the classic movie *Harvey*, James Stewart describes how his imaginary rabbit, Harvey, and he go into a bar and sit down, and pretty soon people turn to him and smile:

> We've entered as strangers. Soon we have friends...they tell about the big, terrible things

they've done and the big, wonderful things
they'll do. Their hopes, their regrets, their loves
and their hates... all very large because nobody
ever brings anything small into a bar.

One could add that no one brings anything small into a counseling
session.

Clubs and coffee shops provide places where people gather, not
so much for the food but for the community with other people.
Afternoon tea, too, provides a break in the monotony or the pressure
of the everyday work schedule. These become places of reprieve,
and as such they are often fiercely defended. Perhaps this is why
men who normally see women as their equals defend the right to
have exclusively male clubs. It is not an issue of equality to them; it
is a matter of defending the sacredness and sameness of this place
that refurbishes them.

After the death of my Aunt Esther I and her husband, my Uncle
Blanton, with whom I had always been close, met together every
Monday night at a coffee shop. Sometimes we ate dinner, but more
often we just had pie and coffee. For him, in particular, it was a
weekly safety zone in which to express grief; for both of us it was a
time to talk over the week and to debate ideas. "Jonesie," as I called
him, had never gone to college, but he had knowledge equal to at
least one Ph.D., and we could go on for hours discussing writing
ideas and Christian theology. The time was a safety zone for both
of us, one that I miss to this day. It was a safety zone of normal life,
for it was not crisis oriented.

* * *

The support of others and the good counsel of caring friends are
what most of us need most of the time. Indeed, for most of us the
question is not whether we will ever be involved in a counseling

situation but rather how formal that counseling will be. There are times, however, when training and skill are required. Then we need the safety zone of more formalized counseling, which still comforts but also deals with the specific problem at hand, like a bout of depression or a troublesome relationship, and goes on to equip us to deal with the world around us from a position of wholeness.

The situations that demand professional counseling are as varied as the individuals involved. Steven was a successful businessman. At his work as a salesman, the demands to perform were heavy. At home his wife's desire for possessions and social status was equally heavy. Both his wife and his boss had quick tempers and tongues. Arguments got Steve nowhere because nasty words and shouting, rather than reason, were the weapons of the day.

After ten days of hospitalization with chest pains, Steven consulted me. Some techniques on how to deal with demanding people were the main focus of the counseling, along with help in building up Steven's low self-image, which had enabled those around him to intimidate him. Steven needed to learn to declare boundaries. The support of friends alone could not have solved Steven's problems.

Lucinda was only five years old, but her mother brought her to see me after she had been diagnosed as having an ulcer. Lucy's parents were divorced, but otherwise she didn't seem to have any unusual negative factors in her environment. Certainly there was nothing that seemed to warrant an ulcer at age five!

During her second appointment, Lucy and I played with a large dollhouse I have in my office. For some children the dollhouse is simply a source of pleasure that relaxes them enough to talk. For others the play is revealing. Lucy focused on the father doll. She moved him upstairs to live. She had the other members of the doll family try to make him feel better. Then, in her play, one night he disappeared, and she explained to me that the doll-father had been murdered.

Translated into real life, it turned out that Lucy's father had indeed disappeared, and Lucy had decided that he had been murdered. When I asked her directly if she felt that her father had been murdered, she replied with a quick yes. Her father did write an occasional letter to his sister, but no one had bothered to tell Lucy, nor had she asked. Once I told her about these letters and she knew that her father was alive, the ulcer vanished. All she needed after that was the love and understanding that her family could best give to her.

Stephanie was a middle-aged woman with crippling fears of almost everything, from standing in line at the bank to sleeping alone at night. Once again her problems and her treatment were unique. For Stephanie the key was in an undiagnosed metabolic imbalance, the diagnosis and treatment of which speeded up the counseling process. Today Stephanie is successful as a teacher, and she can barely relate to her former fears.

* * *

Some people feel that counseling must focus on the past in order to be effective. To the contrary, although the past often gives insight into the present, becoming tangled up in the memories of the past can actually exacerbate a problem rather than relieve it. To know that you fear elevators because you were stuck in one at age three may be interesting for the insight it provides, but from what I have observed, it rarely rids you of the fear.

There are, at times, exceptions. The girl who consulted me regarding her seemingly unfounded hatred for her mother told me a little about her childhood. When she described her father's death from a heart attack, which occurred when she was only ten, she told how she saw her mother give her father some medication within seconds of his death. "She killed him," she exclaimed suddenly, "and I miss my father so much!"

After she had calmed down a little, I pointed out to her that maybe her mother had been trying to save her father's life, not take it. "I never thought of that," she admitted. "My mother and father fought a lot, and I was usually on my father's side. So I thought she killed him." One session with the mother clarified the situation to the girl. Her mother had given her husband a nitroglycerin pill, hoping to stop the attack. The mother and daughter still had problems to work out, but now that was possible. In this case, the basis for the solution was to be found in the past.

When events in the past are troublesome, at times understanding them better in the light of today may be helpful. Yet, more often than not, dwelling on the past just replays, once again, events that were harmful then and are still harmful now. Remembering how you were molested by your uncle, or how your mother didn't believe you when you told her, or how much you resented the favoritism shown to your older brother doesn't usually do much except make you feel as if it were happening all over again. Once again, it's one thing to know that you are afraid of elevators because you were trapped in one at age three. It's quite another thing to cure the fear. The insight is merely interesting. It is not a cure.

For a period of time well after the end of World War II, a number of concentration camp survivors committed suicide. "Why then?" one might ask, a question for which there might be many answers. Yet many of these individuals who killed themselves were historians or writers. One can only wonder if, with the post war revival of interest in World War II and the subsequent references to the atrocities of the camps, for at least these very vocal individuals, the old memories of the past got out of control. "Letting it all hang out" may have stirred up emotions which caused old wounds to open up and fester.

Even though he is viewed as the father of psychoanalysis, Freud himself was the first to acknowledge the limitations of a therapy that analyzed the past. He spoke of the day when dealing with a person's body chemistry would be a pivotal factor in the treatment of emotional disturbances. Then he said, "But for the moment we have nothing better at our disposal than the technique of psychoanalysis, and for that reason, in spite of its limitations, it is not to be despised."[8] Today many of us believe that, apart from or in conjunction with physical treatment of the body, there are quicker and more effective techniques than psychoanalysis that can be used to treat psychological problems.

* * *

In addition to believing that psychological help must be done through analyzing the past, many feel that counseling must be painful in order to work. In contrast, many of the people I see who feel better after their counseling sessions and look forward to them are often the ones who receive the greatest benefit. You don't have to get worse to feel better. I am always pleased when someone leaves my office and says, "I feel so much better than I did when I came in." For some it is the first time that they've ever really noticed a flower in bloom as they walked to their car, or stopped to look up at a cloud formation in the sky. One of the positive fringe benefits of good mental health is freedom to look out from inside oneself to the world around, to see nature, and to feel a oneness with other human beings.

When I was a teenager, I had a remarkable English teacher, Esther Mildred Weinstock, who possessed this kind of appreciation of life. She used to write quotations on the blackboard, and often I copied them into a notepad that I still have. One such quotation expressed the simple joy of ordinary human life and challenged the reader to grasp that ordinariness while it still exists:

Normal day, let me be aware of the treasure you are. Let me learn from you, savor you, bless you before you depart. Let me not pass you by in quest of some rare and perfect tomorrow. Let me hold you while I may, for it will not always be so. One day I shall dig my nails into the earth, or bury my face in the pillow, or stretch myself taut, or raise my hands to the sky, and want more than all the world your return.

– Mary Jane Irion

The growth that occurs in the safety zone of counseling enables human beings to live closer to their highest potential. Moreover, it also frees them from themselves enough to enjoy simple pleasures. It should liberate them from bondage to the recordings of *what if* and *why not*. It should enable them to be free enough of their own self-concerns to care what happens to another human being and to worship God because of who He is, rather than what He can give.

Such growth does not proceed in a straight line. There is no exact formula for wholeness, for each individual person is unique. Change is new, and new is scary. Even good change is scary simply because it is still change. However, it is wonderful to go out from the hearth, this place of safety, feeling better equipped to deal with life. It is wonderful to realize that what we don't like about ourselves we can change and to see, for perhaps the first time, that we have qualities we can truly respect.

Those of us who are Christians believe in the importance of each individual human being. In an eloquent expression of that importance, the singer and actress Ethel Waters said, "My father raped my mother when she was twelve and, you know what, they're dedicating a park to me in Lancaster, Pennsylvania."[9]

A young girl came into my office after her parents had thrown her out. Catharine was bright, capable, and pretty, but all she could say was, "There must be something wrong with me. Even my parents don't want me." Catharine was a young adult by the time I met her, but childhood abuse and neglect had made her feel that she had no worth at all.

Session after session went by. Catharine enjoyed the counseling sessions, but she didn't change. She was sure that even I, if I really knew her, would agree that she was no good.

One afternoon, as she was telling me about her belief in God, I suddenly threw out a question to her: "Do you believe God makes junk?"

"Of course not," she replied indignantly. "God wouldn't do that."

"But He made you," I countered.

There was a long silence. Then a slight grin. The resistance had been broken through. Catharine had started to make her way back from a lifetime of self-hate. The turning point had been her belief in a God who didn't make junk. The setting for that discovery had been a counseling session that, for her, had become a safety zone of discovery, a pathway to wholeness.

That's what counseling is all about.

I often feel very grateful to God that I have undergone fearful depression of spirits. I know the borders of despair, and the horrible brink of that gulf of darkness into which my feet have almost gone; but hundreds of times I have been able to give a helpful grip to brethren and sisters who have come into that same condition, which grip I could never have given if I had not known their deep despondency. So I believe that the darkest and most dreadful experience of a child of God will help him to be a fisher of men if he will but follow Christ. Keep close to your Lord and he will make every step a blessing to you.

– Charles H. Spurgeon

Two

BETWEEN THE EXTREMES

*D*epressed over pressures at work and the problems of a teenage daughter, Jeanine made an appointment for herself and her husband with their pastor. When the couple disagreed, the pastor told Jeanine that he didn't want to hear her point of view, just her husband's. Furthermore, he declared, "Learn to be a submissive wife. Then your depression will go away." Even her husband didn't agree with that approach. The next morning Jeanine was too upset to go to work. Her husband was confused and angry at the pastor. And for him there was a new problem: his boss at work was a close friend of the pastor's. What if he found out about their marital problems? Seeking help had only complicated matters. After all, it wouldn't be the first time that he himself had found out other people's secrets in the form of a prayer request.

Jeanine, on the other hand, was more concerned about her immediate problem: depression. With that in mind she sought the help of another pastor in town. His church was much smaller than the one her family attended. Perhaps he would be more understanding. She was in for an abrupt awakening.

As Jeanine began to explain her feelings of depression to the young pastor, he interrupted her. "People who are depressed have a sin problem," he explained. "This will take some time," he continued. "We will need to go though the whole list!" Completely intimidated Jeanine fled back to her own church where she encountered one of the youth pastors. Reassuring her that depression was not a sin, he urged her to see a professional counselor and gave her a name and a telephone number of one he trusted. It was by that convoluted process that Jeanine came to see me in my counseling office.

* * *

Most people who consider seeking professional counseling find the prospect intimidating. "How do I know who to go to?" is part of the dilemma. For some, especially those in the Christian community, the issue is a moral one: "Is it right for a Christian to seek professional counseling?" or "If I go for help, should I just get pastoral counseling from my church?"

Further complicating the problem, psychotherapy itself is very diverse in scope. Most people don't realize that counseling, or therapy, is not uniformly the same. It can range from helpful and even life preserving to vague, useless, or even dangerous. A variety of methods can be employed which can be consistent with biblical teaching, opposed to Christian beliefs, or neither.

An example of a very unorthodox extreme which I witnessed was the experience of a young man who sought my help. What happened to this young man is illustrative of a whole variety of inappropriate therapies, whether they are used by a Christian counselor or one who is secular.

Ben was young and talented. Yet he was too full of fear to hold down a job. At the same time he was bled out financially from so-called psychological treatment which had offered the pain of a cattle prod to cure his ever-increasing anxiety. Until he ran out of money, in weekly sessions he was told by his therapist to shock himself with a cattle prod every time he got fearful. It didn't work. He just became more fearful. I made a deal with him. I would see him but would postpone payment until he got a job. His question was: "What if I can't ever work again?" "Then we both lose," I replied.

We started therapy and Ben recovered quickly. He got a job, a wife, and eventually a baby. He is probably the only person I never billed but still received regular checks from until what he owed was paid off.

* * *

More often than not bad counseling is not bizarre but is simply petty or inept. After trying marital counseling for four or five sessions a young couple finally quit after they felt it was not working. The therapist seemed a little disgruntled but Bill, the husband, didn't think much about it. Bill was a young attorney with a thriving practice. The day after terminating the counseling, Bill picked up his cell phone messages right before a heavy day in court. There was only one message. The voice was that of his now past therapist. And the message consisted of only one word: "Goodbye!" The therapist had to have the last word, literally. Bemused and a little hurt, Bill sat in silence for a moment. Then, thanking God he had left this man's therapy, Bill left for court.

There are definitely some "crazies" out there in the psychotherapy world, even among those who call themselves Christians. A couple who sought the help of a Christian therapist went several times before the husband realized that the whole focus had been on his wife and her problems. After what turned out to be their last session, standing in front of the office door Joe said to the therapist: "When do I get to address some of *my* issues?" Angrily, the therapist pulled out a small notebook, grabbed a pen and, still frowning, shouted "Okay, talk!"

* * *

In contrast to the previous example and similar to the example of Jeanine, in the more fundamentalist Christian groups there is more often counseling which affirms the needs of men over those of women or children. Some counseling also over spiritualizes problems which produces unrealistic guilt rather than healing and even denies the appropriateness of much needed psychotropic medication. Some, like the "PsychoHeresy" group, apparently even deny the value of counseling in any form and the appropriateness of psychotropic medication as well.

In a "PsychoHeresy Awareness Letter," this group writes: "The wisdom of God needs no assistance when it comes to psychological problems of living...As a matter of fact, adding the imperfect psychological wisdom of man to the perfect wisdom of God actually subtracts from pure wisdom by diminishing, displacing, diluting, and disturbing it."[1] In contrast to this viewpoint, since the Bible speaks much about practical living, sound psychological counseling can provide practical help in putting such principles into shoe leather.

The Bible deals with many subjects ranging from church order to child rearing and living the Christian life. No one would begin to say that sermons which develop and expound on such areas would be "diminishing" the Bible by doing so. It is certainly possible to obtain false teaching through destructive therapy or heretical sermons, but when the therapy or sermons are consistent with Biblical truth, or not against such truth, then to condemn something like therapy as "diminishing" the word of God is to condemn preaching also as minimizing the teaching that "it is all in the Word."

In an atmosphere which forbids the use of psychological counseling or redefines its use, symptoms like depression and anxiety are often considered to be sin. In the words of the so-called Biblical Counseling guru, Jay Adams, "There is no hope in speaking of neuroses, defense mechanisms or repressions; God has not promised to do anything about such problems. But every Christian knows that Jesus came to deal with sin. Labeling sin 'sin' then is kindly because it gives hope; it points to the true problem and to God's salvation. ...Ultimately it [a psychiatric approach] constitutes rebellion against God by the rejection of His Word, His Son and His Spirit as irrelevant or inadequate."[2] Jay Adams' reinforces this thought when he says: "The hope for depressed persons, as elsewhere, lies in this: the depression is the result of the counselee's sin."[3]

* * *

Such an attitude seems to preclude the use of psychotherapy at all. Perhaps due to criticism for ignoring the psychological needs of their followers, fundamentalists have in recent years established a form of counseling which they call Nouthetic or Biblical Counseling. From what I have read and heard, feelings are minimized or ignored, emotional discomfort is relegated to sin, talking about feelings is considered detrimental, and counseling sessions deal with behavior only, not feelings. All of this is in sharp contrast to the Nineteenth Century when Charles H. Spurgeon, a favorite preacher of today's fundamentalists and mine, could stand up in his pulpit and declare that he was down (or depressed) on that occasion. To him his depression was not sin but something which helped him deal with others who were "down." If the history of great men of God is any indication of the incidence of depression among the godly, then rather than being indicative of sinfulness or indifference to God, depression may often be an indicator that God intends to use and bless an individual.

To draw a little more from Spurgeon, even for those who walk closely with their Lord "if the Christian did not sometimes suffer heaviness he would begin to grow too proud, and think too much of himself, and become too great in his own esteem. Those of us who are of elastic spirit, and who in our health are full of everything that can make life happy, are too apt to forget that all our own springs must be in Him...."

For "in heaviness we often learn lessons that we never could attain elsewhere. Do you know that God has beauties for every part of the world; and He has beauties for every place of experience? There are views to be seen from the tops of the Alps that you can never see

elsewhere. Ay, but there are beauties to be seen in the depths of the
dell that ye could never see on the tops of the mountains; there are
glories to be seen on Pisgah, wondrous sights to be beheld when by
faith we stand on Tabor; but there are also beauties to be seen in our
Gethsemanes, and some marvelously sweet flowers to be culled by
the edge of the dens of the leopards. Men will never become great
in divinity until they become great in suffering. 'Ah!' said Luther,
'affliction is the best book in my library,' and let me add, the best
leaf in the book of affliction is that blackest of all the leaves, the
leaf called heaviness, when the spirit sinks within us, and we cannot
endure as we could wish."[4]

* * *

I have found that many who espouse the belief that all negative
emotions like depression and anxiety are sinful show faulty logic
and at times become deceptive in much of their development
of such ideas. For example, in his book *Competent to Counsel*,
Adams' cites several psychiatrists who questioned some of Freud's
teachings and were reputed to have a higher success rate than
most, thus giving them grudging credit. In the example of Dr. G. L.
Harrington, Adams' cites Harrington's work in Los Angeles at the
V. A. Hospital. States Adams': "G. L. Harrington, in a V. A. hospital
in Los Angeles, for example, worked with 210 male patients in
Building 206. Building 206 was the end of the line. All hope for
these men had been given up. Many could not even take care of
their most elemental needs. Previously there had been an average
of only two releases from Building 206 each year, but after the first
year of Harrington's responsibility program, 75 men were released
from the hospital, and the next year he predicted that 200 would be
released – that is, almost a complete turnover."[5]

In spite of his admission of Harrington's success Adams' is still
critical of Harrington's use of the word "Therapy," thereby showing

that even disagreement with Freud and overt success would not change Adams' in his mindset that psychotherapy does not work. To praise a man at the same time you fail to rethink your position defies logic.

Early in my practice G. L. Harrington was one of my mentors. To my way of thinking he was the best of his field. Yes, he disagreed with Freud on a number of issues but that didn't make him stop being a therapist. His father had been a psychiatrist also and G. L., as some called him, had sat on Freud's knee as a small child.

In Adams'' book he never finishes the story about Harrington. He *did* eventually empty out his ward in Building 206. I remember how proud he was one day when he encountered a past patient on the street with his wife and baby. The man was recovered and whole, thanks to Harrington and his therapy. If Adams' wanted to disprove the value of good therapy he picked the wrong man to cite.

Furthermore, even though Dr. Harrington would have been considered to be a "secular" therapist, he did not oppose people's religious beliefs nor did he mock the idea of God. He read several of my books, which were strictly evangelical, and responded with respect.

After my mother was involved in a fatal car accident, which took her life after a few days, I called him. It was the Sunday following the accident which had occurred on Saturday. Since we referred to each other, Dr. Harrington assumed the call was about a patient he had recently referred. When I told him what had happened, there was a long silence.

"You don't need me," he said humbly. "You need God."

"I have God," I replied, "but I still need to sort out my thoughts."

I saw him the next day and found that venting my feelings and sorting out my options was a great help in going on through some very difficult days which followed. Not all secular therapists are opposed to religious belief, nor are all Christian therapists necessarily walking close to God or well trained psychologically – and sometimes training can be the pivotal point in effecting a cure.

* * *

Even Adams' treatment of Freud is not totally accurate. Freud's followers, more than Freud, were responsible for exaggerating Freud's theories and relying on them as absolute truth. With honesty and integrity Freud once admitted: "The future may teach us to exercise a direct influence, by means of particular chemical substances, upon the amounts of energy and their distribution in the apparatus of the mind. It may be that there are other undreamed-of possibilities of therapy. But for the moment we have nothing better at our disposal than the technique of psychoanalysis, and for that reason, in spite of its limitations, it is not to be despised."[6] In later years he added: "I am firmly convinced that one day all these disturbances we are trying to understand will be treated by means of hormones or similar substances."[7]

Much of what Freud said in these statements has begun to come true. Harrington himself was a good example of better techniques, less embedded in the analysis of a patient's past and more focused on current behavior. In the treatment of something like Bipolar Disorder alone there are now choices as to usable medications; whereas when I started my practice Lithium was the only acceptable treatment – and before Lithium the patient was always at risk since talk therapy could rarely effectively treat the disorder. Perhaps we need to look back at the Scriptures and more honestly apply what we read. For example, "Let your moderation be known to all men." The challenge is to be people of balance.

* * *

Among those who practice Nouthetic or Biblical counseling, two broad problems exist: the inability to see emotional problems apart from spiritual problems, along with the mistaken idea that all Christian therapists promote biblical principles, and that non-Christian therapists attempt to destroy their patients' Christianity. In contrast, from my own acquaintance with psychotherapists, the good ones do not try to discourage their patients' Christian beliefs. Furthermore, while a competent Christian therapist is certainly ideal for a Christian who has problems, I have encountered a number of Christian therapists who are confused spiritually and not very proficient psychologically. Although many people, Christian and non-Christian, have had some deplorable experiences with psychotherapists, from what I hear in my office, that experience has been true of both Christian *and* non-Christian therapists. There are more non-Christian therapists than Christian, and many of them are very effective, just as are many secular lawyers, doctors, and plumbers.

Also, some Christians seem to feel that Christian therapists are the only ones who demand a sense of responsibility from a person, hence the need for a Christian counselor who will not downgrade the patients' standards. Inherent again here is the idea that low standards and sin are at the root of most emotional problems. To view secular therapy as consistently anti-Christian is an attitude which is often based on ignorance or on some older forms of psychoanalysis and on a few far-out therapies which are on the fringes of more responsible therapy.

* * *

Perhaps of even greater concern for any Christian who wants sound counseling should be that which is connected to certain groups within the so-called Emerging Church. The Emergent Church, a faction of the Emerging Church which has abandoned basic and essential Christian doctrine, with or without its implications in psychotherapy, is one of the most dangerous factors in the organized Christian Church today. Theology is based on experience and can vary according to whose experience seems important at any given time or place. To some the deity of Christ and the Second Coming are in question. Furthermore, many believe another "God" could replace the Christ of Christianity. To a few, Christianity itself may have outlived its day. Thus to the Emergents the Kingdom of God is here on earth now, which explains the heightened emphasis on humanitarian endeavors. Thus, as in most movements, there are wide variations within the Emerging Church. Some are simply deep into experience and an overemphasis on the inner being, while others go to the full extreme of a denial of Biblical Christianity.

Whereas the word "spiritual" used to be an innocent expression of a desire to know God, it now acts as a red flag.

> What it means exactly when a person declares himself or herself to be "spiritual but not religious" is a matter of some debate....

> One thing that it *does* signify, almost universally, is the rejection of traditional faiths as a primary source of connection to the divine.[8]

Just as so-called "Biblical Counseling" is not always sound biblically, some therapies related to the Emerging Church thinking are even less biblical. Combining a strange mixture of worship of self, finding help within yourself, and forming theological beliefs out of mystical experience alone is not indicative of sound Christianity. Not unlike a basic tenet of Hinduism, some even attempt to mix together various forms of religious thought into a conglomeration of what feels good *for me*. Out of body experiences, trances, excessive meditation and various forms of prayer can all be used as tools.

As one "Christian" therapist said to me: "You mean you don't throw people into trances?" At least he used the correct word for what he was describing. The current emphasis on "centering prayer" and "contemplative prayer," both as an exercise in the church and in the counseling office, is more subtle and characterizes what I consider to be a dangerous threat to biblical Christianity today.

In the times in which we live with instant news, a plethora of new technology, disposable goods, and a highly mobile lifestyle, quietness is rare. Yet to be quiet before God is a biblical principle.

A teenage girl, non-Christian and way into drugs, once said to me: "I like to go to church when the building is empty. The music is better at my rock concerts and sometimes all the church activity is just boring. But when I'm alone I can try to find God." She valued a quiet place to seek God. Entertainment could be more easily found outside of the church.

Especially in the taking of communion we need quietness and time to worship God for who He is. In times of conflict and for just everyday living we need times of quietness to pray and to read the Bible and to think about what God is trying to tell us. An old hymn by E. May Grimes says it well:

> Speak, Lord, in the stillness,
>   While I wait on Thee;
> Hushed my heart to listen
>   In expectancy.
>
> Speak, O blessed Master,
>   In this quiet hour,
> Let me see Thy face, Lord,
>   Feel Thy touch of power.
>
> For the words Thou speakest,
>   "They are life" indeed;

Living Bread from heaven,
  Now my spirit feed!

All to Thee is yielded,
  I am not my own;
Blissful, glad surrender
  I am Thine alone.

Speak, Thy servant heareth!
  Be not silent, Lord:
Waits my soul upon Thee
  For the quickening word!

Fill me with the knowledge
  Of Thy glorious will;
All Thine own good pleasure
  In Thy child fulfill.[9]

There is nothing wrong with meditation upon God. There is a lot wrong, however, with seeking mystical experience for its own sake, and there is something very dangerous in trying to create out-of-body experiences or trances.

In a tone which sounds like it has been greatly influenced by Eastern thought, and which seems to go beyond the kind of meditation which the Scriptures teach, in his book *Open Mind, Open Heart*, when Thomas Keating writes about centering prayer, he advises us to choose a so-called sacred word and then to "close our eyes to let go of what is going on around and within us. We introduce the sacred word inwardly and as gently as laying a feather on a piece of absorbent cotton." Then, continues Keating: "'When you become aware of thoughts, return ever-so-gently to the sacred word'...By 'returning ever-so-gently to the sacred word,' a minimum of effort is indicated. This is the only activity we initiate during the time of centering prayer. During the course of our prayer, the sacred word may become vague or even disappear...."

The minimum time for this prayer is twenty minutes. Two periods are recommended each day, one first thing in the morning and one in the afternoon or early evening."[10] In my opinion the trance-like state one is left in as the word disappears is dangerous both psychologically and spiritually.

In a strange mixture of the East and Christian thinking, Psalm 46:10 is often distorted. "Be still and know that I am God" does not imply trances, nor does it validate New Age guru Deepak Chopra when he sometimes refers to the silence penetrating into your very soul.

In *Finding Grace at the Center*, Keating and Pennington have effectively stated the connection between what is happening as the philosophy of the East merges with "Christian" thinking:

> We should not hesitate to take the fruit of the age-old wisdom of the East and "capture" it for Christ. Indeed, those of us who are in ministry should make the necessary effort to acquaint ourselves with as many of these Eastern techniques as possible.
>
> Many Christians who take their prayer life seriously have been greatly helped by Yoga, Zen, TM and similar practices, especially where they have been initiated by reliable teachers and have a solidly developed Christian faith to find inner form and meaning to the resulting experiences.[11]

More blatantly, Rob Bell, a graduate of Wheaton College and someone promoted by some so-called evangelical churches, wrote: "We're rediscovering Christianity as an Eastern religion, as a way of life."[12]

Going one step further, Tony Jones defines the confusion which exists:

> I'm asked a lot, "What is it that folks in the emerging church have in common?" People ask that because it's become clear that there's no statement of faith, no common set of practices, no denominational boundaries that quite capture the breadth of movement.[13]

I would restate at this point that the above statement, in my opinion, declares the position of the Emergent Church rather than that of others in the so-called Emerging Church where beliefs vary greatly.

At another radical extreme, Barry Taylor writes: "Whether 'Christianity' has any future at all as a vibrant expression of faith in the Man from Galilee is a matter of debate as far as I am concerned. Perhaps the times call for something else, something other, not merely the repackaging of old metaphors (playing the "relevant" game), but a new incarnation of what it means to follow Jesus." Again he states: "I have already raised the notion that there may not be a future for 'Christianity,' the religion of Christian faith."[14] Getting to the root of the departure from biblical doctrine another writer says:

> Is our religion the only one that understands the true meaning of life? Or does God place his truth in others too?...The gospel is not *our* gospel, but the gospel of the kingdom of God, and what belongs to the kingdom of God cannot be hijacked by Christianity.[15]

Thus consistent in much emergent writing is that doctrine grows out of experience rather than the other way around.

* * *

Error is rarely new. Usually it is recycled. In II Timothy Paul warns the Church against "profane *and* vain babblings; for they will increase unto more ungodliness. And their word will eat as doth a gangrene, of whom are Hymenæus and Philetus, Who, concerning the truth, have erred, saying that the resurrection is past already; and overthrow the faith of some." (II Timothy 2:16-18) In a commentary on these verses a number of decades ago, H.C.G. Moule wrote:

> What their 'profane,' secular, unspiritual 'babblings' were, we can only guess, but the reference to a 'resurrection past already' helps us in guessing. It is likely that we have here one of the earliest allusions to a type of thought known later as Gnosticism...the religion of 'Knowledge' rather than of Faith; a teaching which claimed to lead its disciple past the common herd of mere *believers* to a superior and gifted circle who should *know* the mysteries of being, and who by such *knowing* should live emancipated from the spirit of matter, ranging at liberty in the world of spirit.
>
> More than probably such was the sense in which, according to this school, 'resurrection had already taken place.' The initiated soul, immaterial *and therefore pure,* by the 'knowledge' – not of self, or sin, or of a holy God, but – of a mystic secret, was held to have soared aloft out of the bondage of matter into a transcendental upper air; not to be partaker there of the bliss of sanctity and love, but – to be released from limitations. Some disciples of the school put

their theory into practice by turning fiercely on the body and punishing it as evil, *because material....*

So these 'advanced' thinkers 'advanced to more and more of impiety,' on principle. So 'their word did eat yet further in, like a gangrene,' creeping from limb to limb of the moral being. 'Their God was their belly, their end was destruction, their glory was in their shame' (Phil. iii. 19).

Is the beacon-fire of that experience unneeded now? Never perhaps since Christianity dawned upon the world was the mental and moral air so thick as it is to-day with thoughts which claim to 'emancipate' man from the *low level* and the *narrow views* of the Gospel of the Cross. Philosophies which, equipped with the newest knowledge of nature, only go back to pagan types of speculation; dark teachings, mainly conveyed in secret, about unseen powers, and about a life other than that shewn to us in Scripture, beyond the veil of death; these things in a thousand forms are everywhere about us. Let us draw only the closer to the LORD, as men who know themselves, and HIM; and let us hold fast *the Word*.[16]

Gnosticism was the error which so attacked the Church at Colossae, which is why Paul warned that group of believers to

Let no one have his own way in robbing you of your prize, your crown of life and joy at the Coming of the Lord, in the way of humility, (the artificial humility of the trained devotee, a

self-abasement before unlawful objects, not the
true humility of a soul at the feet of Jesus,) **and
worship of angels**, the unauthorized *cultus* of
those who are but the Lord's "ministering spirits"
for His people's good; **invading things**, regions,
which he has not seen, getting inanely inflated
(present participle) **by the** mere **mind of his
flesh**, the unconsecrated exercise of thought
in the unregenerate state; wandering afar in
speculations and imaginations which have not
God but man for origin, and which therefore
cannot humble, chasten, hallow, the thinker,
but can only inflate him in his own esteem; **and
not holding fast**, in his faith and in his teaching,
the Head; the blessed Lord who is (i. 18) "the
Head of the body, the Church," in all things pre-
eminent, vitally and for ever necessary to His
followers for both life and light...[17]

In summary Moule aptly quotes: "Angels will always win the day
over Jesus Christ despised and crucified, if the choice of a mediator...
is left to the vanity of the human mind."[18] Then he warns once
again: "Have you in you a secret of life and development which
is nothing less than God? Have not your new teachers manifestly
travelled, and sought to lead you, to a lower level, and to a remoter
distance from that blessed Centre? Then be on the watch against all
that they would teach as their distinctive message."[19]

* * *

Once again, the Emerging Church influence can range from a
strongly evangelical stand which is strictly biblical but culturally
adaptive, as Mark Driscoll of Mars Hill in Seattle has apparently

become, to radical departure from biblical theology. In Driscoll's experience, "Mars Hill has become an anomaly. With its sheer size and orthodox theology – far more conservative than most other emerging churches – it no longer fits neatly into that niche."[20]

In another context Driscoll clearly states his position:

> Not only must God's people personally believe the gospel of Jesus Christ, but they also must publicly contend for it. This is because the gospel is under continual attack by Satan, the "father of lies," and a seemingly endless army of false teachers, false prophets, false shepherds, and false apostles, whom he sends to wage war against the church. The New Testament letters model a warrior's battle cry, declaring that heretics are: dogs and evildoers, empty and deceitful, puffed up without reason, given to mythical speculation and vanity without understanding, products of a shipwrecked faith, demonic liars with seared consciences, peddlers of silly myths, arrogant fools with depraved minds, the spiritual equivalent of gangrene, foolish and ignorant, chatty deceivers, destructive blasphemers, ignorantly unstable, and antichrists.
>
> In our day of pluralistic, postmodern, perspectival politeness, the terse language of Peter and Paul seems narrowly intolerant, as if they had never been enlightened by taking a philosophy of religion class at a community college from a long-haired, self-medicated grad student. Nonetheless, the truth is the truth, and

Peter, Paul, and many of the faithful who have followed Christ on the narrow road of truth have seen their blood spilled by those who were as brotherly as Cain for contending the truth.[21]

* * *

If defining the Emerging Church is difficult, showing its connection to psychotherapy is equally challenging. The focus of some in the Emerging Church on contemplative prayer crosses the boundary between Church and therapy, theology and professional counseling. In my opinion clinical psychologist Larry Crabb has been instrumental in crossing that boundary. In his book *The Papa Prayer* Crabb says:

> I've practiced centering prayer. I've contemplatively prayed. I've prayed liturgically. I've interceded and petitioned. The first model of prayer I learned as a kid was ACTS: adoration, confession, thanksgiving, supplication. I tried that, too, for years. I've benefited from each, and I still do."[22]

And again: "Other forms of relating to God that have unique value in connecting us to Him include contemplative prayer and centering prayer."[23]

In a *Christianity Today* article in 2003 Crabb says that he now believes that "in today's church, therapy should be replaced by another, more ancient practice – 'spiritual direction.'"[24]

Enabling this process has been the current emphasis on taking psychotherapy out of the hands of trained counselors and entrusting it to a sort of lay counseling within the church. Then as the church, particularly the Emergent Church, takes control of counseling it is only natural that a variety of Eastern influences and techniques are employed.

Crabb's spiritual direction involves a director and a directee. The director, who is not necessarily a trained professional, helps the directee get closer to God. The primary emphasis is not on solving any psychological or clinical problems. Personally, from that point of view, I see little difference between this approach and the Biblical Counseling approach except that while it is perhaps kinder, in some cases it is less pristine in doctrine, and it may employ the use of some Eastern practices.

As to the goal of counseling, in an interview published in *Christianity Today* Crabb states: "As spiritual directors, we need to encourage people not to see brokenness as an unnatural state. Rather than trying to pull someone out of his brokenness back into our world, we need to jump into his brokenness and meet him at the place where God is working."[25] Consistent with the previous statement, in another interview Crabb states that "symptom relief" is the "lesser goal."[26] Yet "symptom relief" is what people seek in therapy and legitimately so. If God chooses to use it for greater growth than just symptomatic relief we rejoice. But let us not minimize pain. To use the thinking of C. S. Lewis in a brief paraphrase, once people have gotten rid of their psychological baggage then they are better equipped to make life decisions. If pain is required as a motivator, leave that to God. We have no right in our counseling with people to do anything but try to alleviate it.

Without the problems of trances, out of body experiences, deep meditation and all the other accoutrements of the Emergent Church, therapy in the church has built-in problems relating to issues of confidentiality and privacy. In the current mode where the counselors are untrained but "intuitive," the problems increase. Perhaps the fad will pass, but once again issues like these tend to recycle again another day.

* * *

For many of us an integrative or dimensional type of therapy seems to work best. For ten years Susan, a teacher respected in the community, had been secretly beaten by her husband. Sometimes it was a slap across the face; at other times she was beaten until she had multiple bruises and was forced to wear long sleeves and pants to cover them. Toward the end of the ten years the violence seemed to escalate to the point where Susan began to fear for her life. Greg was a leader in the church they attended so she was afraid no one there would believe her, especially since she had never complained before. Furthermore, Greg had threatened her very life if she talked. For one thing she was grateful: her long wished for pregnancy had never happened. At least he could never hurt a child of their conception.

Then one night after church Greg came home angry. "Why can't you clean this house?" he screamed as he looked around the room and observed a coat draped across the chair and a pair of shoes not yet put away. He was angry and only too happy to throw that anger at the one person he knew who would not retaliate and who was too afraid to judge him.

This time the beating was even more severe than usual and when it was over Susan knew that she probably had at least one broken rib. Almost immobilized by pain she watched as Greg came to her with the obvious intention of having sex.

"No," she cried out. "I'm hurt."

"You deserve it, you bitch," he screamed back. With that statement, Greg proceeded to force sex and then, satisfied, he left the house as Susan lay writhing in pain.

Crawling painfully to the phone, Susan dialed 911 for medical help. In the next days and weeks Susan's body slowly recovered and Greg was arrested and charged. But the emotional and spiritual wounds were harder to heal.

She filed for divorce but was told by members of her church that divorce would be a sin. Furthermore, why had she stayed with this abusive man was a question which plagued even her. About that time she sought professional counseling and ended up in my office.

Her counseling was a perfect example of what I like to call Dimension Therapy. Every aspect of her being – body, mind, and spirit – needed help. And each of these parts had various dimensions. For example, on the physical level she had two broken ribs and she was malnourished from years of neglecting her body. Spiritually, she was disillusioned in a church which didn't support her when she needed it.

Psychological factors were the most serious long range. A damaged self esteem had made her feel that she wasn't worth anyone better than Greg, and years of abuse had only increased that feeling. Her self hate showed in how she dressed and in a low grade anger and distrust with even those who supported her. The practical dimensions of dressing attractively, in essence improving how she looked, added to the challenge of entertaining friends in a way that nurtured positive relationships and helped in alleviating her guilt over her divorce, all converged to strengthen a more positive view of herself. Also the divorce issue overlapped into the spiritual dimension. Since the Bible speaks of adultery as the basis for divorce, and since the Greek word for adultery in the references relating to divorce is a more general term meaning sexual sin, Susan did have a biblical basis. Forced sex after physical abuse can hardly be called anything but rape, even in a marriage union.

* * *

People vary in their needs. Some have a strong spiritual life but have psychological areas which need help. Others may have physical limitations. Frequently, the needs overlap. A person with cancer, for example, may need help with Post Traumatic Stress.

A husband who cheats on his wife will probably have a need for both psychological and spiritual treatment. And within each of the three basic components of body, mind, and spirit there are many dimensions which may or may not contribute to the overall problem.

Dimension Therapy is similar to integrative therapy in that it acknowledges the fact that sound psychology and biblical principles are not in conflict with each other. Both would also include treatment of the body, mind, and spirit.

Dimension Therapy, however, goes on to stress more specifically that man is multidimensional. Within the scope of body, mind, and spirit there are many dimensions or levels, any of which might need treatment for any given individual at any time. Furthermore, during one's lifetime a person may experience various problems resulting from a variety of causes in the body or mind or spirit, or from any combination within the three.

Indeed a person's body, mind, and spirit make up a totality in which one or the other may emerge predominantly at any given time. A woman going through menopause may experience periods of depression which should not be labeled as primarily psychological or spiritual. She may derive help from spiritual or psychological sources, but the primary cause is physical. Certain drugs are now being used effectively with some forms of mental illness, further validating the biochemical basis for many emotional problems.

A person's spiritual life, too, may be directly affected by his physical and emotional state, a state which may fluctuate from time to time. It is often more difficult to feel spiritually strong when you feel physically or psychologically weak, for example. Esau sold his birthright, not when he was physically strong, but when he was exhausted and hungry. Peter denied Christ under the duress of a young girl's mockery.

* * *

The idea that we are a composite of body, mind, and spirit is not new by any means. The Bible says that "A cheerful heart does good like medicine" (Prov. 17:22), implying a relationship between the body and the mind. In Proverbs 15:30 we read, "Pleasant sights and good reports give happiness and health." "Hope deferred makes the heart sick" (Prov. 13:12). "Reverence for God gives a man deep strength" (Prov. 14:26).

More recently than biblical times and yet a century ago, Charles H. Spurgeon, a man still well known and esteemed for his godliness, preached a remarkable sermon. He said:

> It is not necessary to prove by quotations from the biographies of eminent ministers that seasons of fearful prostration have fallen to the lot of most if not all of them. The life of Luther might suffice to give a thousand instances and he was by no means of the weakest sort. His great spirit was often in the seventh heaven of exultation, and as frequently on the borders of despair.[27]

As to the reason for such despair, Spurgeon goes on to relate the mind, body, and spirit:

> Certain bodily maladies are fruitful fountains of despondency. And let a man strive as he may against their influence, there will be hours and circumstances in which they will overcome him.
>
> As for mental maladies, is any man altogether sane? Are we not all a little off balance? Some

minds appear to have a gloomy tinge essential to their individuality....

These infirmities may be no detriment to a man's career of usefulness. They may even have been imposed upon him by divine wisdom as a necessary qualification for his peculiar course of service...[28]

Then, rather than overspiritualizing emotional problems and denying that Christians should ever have any, Spurgeon continues in quite an opposite view:

But where in body and mind there are predisposing causes to lowness of spirit, it is no marvel if in dark moments the heart succumbs to them. The wonder in many cases is—and if inner lives could be written, men would see it so—how some keep at their work at all and still wear a smile upon their countenance. Grace has its triumphs and patience its martyrs, martyrs none the less to be honored because flames kindle about their spirits rather than their bodies, and their burning is unseen by human eyes...[29]

Without question there can be any number of psychological causes for the emotional problems which confront people. However, in most cases both the cause and the cure should not be disconnected from the physical and the spiritual. More important for Christians to realize is that, while help in handling emotional problems will certainly be found in a relationship with Christ, the complete answer may not be spiritual at all. This realization will save many a Christian from feeling guilt over his or her emotional problems and will prevent some Christians from sinning by self-righteous judgment of others.

* * *

In "The American Scholar" Ralph Waldo Emerson discusses the paradox of the whole having several parts and yet being one.

> It is one of those fables which out of an unknown antiquity conveys an unlooked-for wisdom, that the gods, in the beginning, divided Man into men, that he might be more helpful to himself; just as the hand was divided into fingers, the better to answer its end.

> This old fable covers a doctrine ever new and sublime; that there is One Man—present to all particular men only partially, or through one faculty; and that you must take the whole society to find the whole man. Man is not a farmer, or a professor, or an engineer, but he is all. Man is priest, and scholar, and statesman, and producer, and solder.[30]

To take Emerson's idea one step further, any one individual is not divided neatly into three parts but is a total of all three. A loaf of bread is made up of several ingredients, such as flour and eggs and milk. Each is distinct from the others, but once they are combined into a loaf of bread they cease to be distinct and separate. Instead of being eggs, flour, and milk, they become bread. Likewise a person is not just three equal parts – body, mind, and spirit – but a whole made up of all three. In spite of this interrelationship, at times one part may stand out from the others, and here the loaf of bread analogy stops.

In her wonderful book *Rose From Briar* Amy Carmichael quotes briefly from *The Spirit of Discipline* by Bishop Paget:

"There is a deep and wonderful prophecy in that inscrutable interaction of soul and body which may sometimes startle, or bewilder, or distress us; it hints at the hope of the body, the opportunity of the soul; it means that the body also is accessible to the Divine life; that there are avenues by which the power of the Resurrection can invade it; that it is capable of a transfiguration; that for it too the Lord from heaven is a quickening Spirit." And he speaks of our very bodies being affected by a real energy from the indwelling of the Spirit of Christ, so that the power of His resurrection may extend even to the physical conditions of our life, "that very slowly and partially, it may be, with limits that are soon reached, and hindrances that will not yield, yet, for all that, very truly and practically, the redemption of our body may be begun on earth."[31]

* * *

We are a long way from the day when people only went to therapists when they completely broke down; yet vestiges of that feeling remain. Fortunately the field of psychotherapy has improved, and the combination of psychotherapy, medical treatment, and spiritual help is becoming more common. Along with these changes the average person has become a little more sophisticated about psychological needs and treatment which has enabled more people to get more help.

Rather than being a godless force used to seduce Christians from their faith, counseling can be a God-given, God-used tool to help

Christians and non-Christians with emotional problems. The human personality is very delicate and vulnerable; yet the same capacity for destruction is also present for growth. The skillful therapist takes that capacity and uses it to shape and strengthen a good self-image. Sometimes change is slow and almost imperceptible, but perhaps it is then all the more rewarding.

A psychologist in the children's ward at a state hospital had been working for a number of months with an autistic six-year-old boy, Mike. At first, Mike could only relate to inanimate objects like airplanes or boats. Then as time passed by, he became aware of some living things, such as butterflies. And part of the therapy sessions involved chasing countless butterflies, and eventually birds, that were never caught.

Yet Mike was still trapped in an imaginary world of his own. Unable to even accept his own identity, he referred to himself as "Mike," never as "I" or "me." He would say, "Mike wants water" or "Mike is tired." Nor could he relate enough to other human beings to even gain direct eye contact. Instead he would look through them or around them, never at them. His growth in connecting with the reality of the world around him was slow.

Then one day after an exhausting chase around the grounds of the institution, Mike and the therapist collapsed on the grass to rest. As he turned toward the therapist, suddenly Mike's eyes focused directly into the therapist's. He said, "*I* see you in *my* eyes, Mr. Wiest." Such can be the miracle of therapy.

My anxieties have anxieties.

– Charlie Brown

Psychiatrist Dr. Susan Vaughan has argued that the talking cure works by "talking to neurons," and that an effective psychotherapist or psychoanalyst is a "microsurgeon of the mind" who helps patients make needed alterations in neuronal networks.

– Norman Doidge, M.D.,
The Brain That Changes Itself

THREE

CUT AND REFOCUS

*L*ast night was not a good night for sleep. We had lightning, thunder, and a rainstorm, which is somewhat unusual for California, after which the humidity immediately soared. Then, just as I was about to turn out my reading light, a car alarm went off that sounded as if it was right under my bedroom window. Usually when that happens on the street where I live, the owner recognizes his or her alarm and goes out and turns it off. Not this time. The grating sound blared into the quiet of the night for a good five minutes or more. Then it stopped abruptly, and I fell asleep.

Two hours of blissful rest went by rapidly. Then, once again the silence of the night was broken with the abrasive noise of the same car alarm. Once again it went its lengthy course and eventually stopped. In another hour the cycle repeated itself.

The real irritation came when it went off at about 4:30 A.M. Early in the night was bad enough. Like most people, I hate waking up in the early hours of the morning most of all, because at that time it is very hard to go back to sleep.

Each time, and especially at 4:30 A.M., when the car alarm went off, certain thoughts, certain tapes or recorded messages, started to play in my mind. It was as though someone pushed the on button of a recorder, leaving me to push the off button, if I wished.

What if that noise continues all night? What if I can't go back to sleep? How can anyone be so selfish? I bet the owner is sleeping peacefully somewhere, while his car alarm wakes me up. Then, the big one: *What if tomorrow is ruined, all because of a stupid car alarm?* I need not remind my reader that thoughts of *what if* do not lead to a good night's sleep or, indeed, to any sleep at all.

This time, however, I did something different from what I would have done a few years back. No amount of anger or logic that I generated was going to affect the owner of that car alarm. I couldn't make him or her turn it off. All I could do was cut the mental recordings of *what if*, realize that the alarm would, indeed, stop in due time, and then focus away from all the disturbing thoughts. The result was that each time I awakened, I went right back to sleep. I didn't waste an extra minute on *what if* and *how could they*.

This morning, while I was drinking my morning coffee, I called a friend on the phone. "I need a simple, clear example on negative mental recordings," I explained, "but I can't think of one." Then I told her about my night with the car alarm. We both went silent and then said simultaneously, "That's it! The car alarm!"

* * *

A mental recording is a repetitive thought or memory that consumes us and only tightens its hold as we try to think our way out of it. The process of playing such a recording ends up, at its worst, with our being tangled up in all kinds of loose recordings that only get more tangled as we struggle against them. Ultimately our recordings can become dream blockers instead of dream builders. Dealing with these negative emotions is a vital dimension of good mental health.

When one of my shelties, Horace, was a small puppy, he seemed to be drawn toward long cords. Inevitably he would get tangled up in them. One day I came home from my office to an utterly silent apartment. Now, anyone who knew Horace at all knew that it was impossible to get into my apartment without either his squeals of delight or his bark of warning. Horace was not a quiet dog.

I searched through every room and called his name. Still, no Horace. Then I noticed that the phone in my bedroom was on the floor and that the receiver and the cord were under the bed. As I got down on the floor and peered under the bed, I saw Horace. He was a frozen mass of fear, sitting upright with the telephone cord wrapped several times around his neck. He didn't move an inch or make a sound, even when he saw me. Then, as I untangled him from the cord, he nestled into my arms and shook with fear.

Horace knew when he was in danger, and so he stopped moving. That saved his life on more than one occasion. Sometimes we humans are not as smart as Horace. We play the recordings of hurtful memories of the past, the *what ifs* of the future, and the frustration of the present until the recordings tangle and threaten our emotional well-being. We keep moving and fighting and analyzing and rethinking until, at times, life itself seems hopeless.

In his book *Painting as a Pastime*, Winston Churchill comments on the words of a psychologist:

> "Worry is a spasm of the emotion; the mind catches hold of something and will not let it go." It is useless to argue with the mind in this condition. The stronger the will, the more futile the task. One can only gently insinuate something else into its convulsive grasp. And if this something else is rightly chosen, if it is really attended by the illumination of another field of interest, gradually, and often quite swiftly, the old undue grip relaxes and the process of recuperation and repair begins.

Churchill claimed that the key to what I call cutting the mental recordings was change:

> It is not enough merely to switch off the lights which play upon the main and ordinary field of interest; a new field of interest must be illuminated. It is no use saying to the tired

> "mental muscles" – if one may coin such an expression – "I will give you a good rest," "I will go for a long walk," or "I will lie down and think of nothing." The mind keeps busy just the same. If it has been weighing and measuring, it goes on weighing and measuring. If it has been worrying, it goes on worrying. It is only when new cells are called into activity…that relief, repose, refreshment are afforded.1

In brief, the solution for turning off old recordings is to cut and refocus, and the process must be lifelong. Old recordings are not eradicated; they are simply controlled. At any given moment they are there again, turned on by a line of music from the past, a whiff of perfume that reminds us of someone we used to know, or news of an alarming incident that ignites our fears like a match lighting up dry grass.

Winston Churchill's interest in cutting such recordings began after he left the Admiralty in 1915. He remained a member of the cabinet and of the war council; and thus, in practical terms, Churchill continued to know everything that was going on but was no longer empowered to act on that knowledge. He knew too much, could do too little, and had too much leisure in which to contemplate the *what ifs* of the nation. It was then that he discovered a great diversion in painting. As he capriciously stated it, he "took a joy ride in a paint box."[2] The result for Churchill was that "whatever the worries of the hour or the threats of the future, once the picture has begun to flow along, there is no room for them in the mental screen."[3] Churchill had discovered a major psychological dimension of mental health, saying "No" to negative mental messages.

Cutting recordings, however, does not mean that we never think about our problems. Indeed, constructive thinking is one very positive step in problem solving. In an interview with Ruth Bell

Graham, Ruth wisely advised balance: "I roll it on the Lord but at the same time I'm searching the Scriptures for comfort.... I'm wanting to learn what He has to teach me through the experience."

She went on to talk compassionately about some of the deep hurts in life that people experience, like the pain of those left behind when a loved one commits suicide, and the need to give people time to heal after such a deep hurt. However, she spoke with balance of the need to go on once the time for healing is past, even in those situations where we may never completely be the same because of the depth of the hurt that has been inflicted. She advised, "'Make the least of all that goes and the most of all that comes,' as the old saying goes. And keep looking forward; don't look backwards."

Balance is indeed required in dealing with emotional pain. To think and talk and work out solutions to problems is a vital part of mental health. When the constructive aspect of thinking is past, however, and a tense, frantic replaying of the same old thoughts begins, then we are simply playing old mental recordings for which *cut and refocus* remain the simplest answers.

* * *

Each of us has old, negative thoughts that block dream building. Sometimes they revolve around old memories – that a parent didn't love us enough, that we failed to go to college, or that we didn't marry the right person. Unfortunately, some memories of the past can be exacerbated even in the counseling process. The *whys* of the past and the thoughts of past hurt can be played and examined until the ghosts of the past and the fears of the future take on the power of a present reality that they do not truly possess. When this happens, progress forward is blocked.

In recent years, because of our national focus on the subject, adults who remember acts of sexual abuse or violence inflicted on them in childhood have seemed uniquely tempted and even advised by certain professionals to think that if they just look harder at the past and try to figure out why it all happened they will somehow feel better. In my opinion, they generally feel worse until they finally walk away from the past and begin to live in the present at the same time they build their dreams for the future.

To a degree, bringing out the past helps make sense of the present, but more often than not the old recordings are played without resolution. Worse still, imagined wrongs that never happened are conjured up. After all, regardless of the cause of our problems, each of us must still take life as it is now while we change the present and try to shape the future.

A young college student came back to see me for the first time since she had last had counseling sessions with me in her early childhood. After we greeted each other, Sara asked me, "Do you have any idea why I am so bossy? Apart from being bossy, things are going well. But my friends get upset with me because I'm always telling them what to do."

I paused and remembered her as a little girl of five. She was tiny then, and yet behind those delicate features had been a stubbornness that had helped her survive as she protected her three-year-old sister and baby brother during their parents' drunken brawls. Bossy had been the appropriate response then. Now it was hurting her. What had worked then was destructive now.

Sara remembered some of the past. Gently I filled in the gaps. At the end of a half hour or so, she smiled and said tearfully, "I understand why. Now, how do I change?" From that time on, our counseling sessions focused on how she could change in the present. Almost her whole family is different now. They've grown individually, and consequently their relationships with each other are improved. It was good for Sara to understand the past and then to cut the past recordings. To play them again would only block the dreams of Sara's future. It was time to go on.

* * *

In dealing with memories of the past, both bad and good, mystery writer Margaret Millar aptly compares the nature of these memories of the past to a closet full of old clothes. She introduces the concept of choice as it relates to dealing with these memories:

> The past was dead and dear, it couldn't change, it didn't threaten. Comfortable and pleasant, like a closet full of old clothes. You could wear some of them when you were alone, but you didn't have to bother with the rest, even to look at them.

> Some of the clothes were ugly with sagging seams, and evil stains, tattered, too loose or too tight. Leave these in the closet. Bring out the yellow linen dress and slip it over your head. See how thick the cloth was and how well it fitted. It made you twenty again.[4]

Choice is indeed an overlooked factor in playing old recordings. We don't have to play them. Sometimes we take out the more painful memories from the past and try to learn from them, or with the positive recordings of the past, we may enjoy savoring them. But sometimes when we play them we don't cut off in time, and they speed out of control until we begin to feel as though the whole past scene were happening all over again. The ghosts in the cemetery seem to take form as if they were real, and it becomes difficult to remember that they are, after all, still ghosts. It is as if things had never changed. In the words of a Holocaust survivor, "The memories are so strong that they can annihilate the present, and that is a grave danger."[5] In times like these a form of self talk within our thinking can help us see these recordings for what they really are and make the choice to take control.

In contrast, but sharing with equal force the power of choice over memories, a friend of mine who was also a survivor of the Holocaust wrote of certain past events he had forgotten: "I do not believe the gaps represent repressed traumas that have to be dug up and reexamined. I believe that one of nature's greatest gifts is our ability to forget."[6] Joseph chose to go on to build his dreams; and his life as an old man was a monument to his success in doing just that.

Sometimes we choose to cut the recordings of the past, but we become overly concerned with frustration regarding the present. Discontent over living in a small house, disappointment over the failure of our children in school, or feelings of inadequacy regarding our careers: all these can become recordings we play that choke out almost all our joy.

Like the past, the future seems to provide a particularly fertile source for negative recordings. Some of us fear old age, helplessness, poverty, and loneliness. Others of us wonder more specifically what we will do if our spouses die before we do or how we will handle a major illness. Some fear death. Others simply get tangled up on the more immediate future, like the next job promotion or the lack of it.

The recordings of the future, like all other recordings, have the potential to get out of control and become dream blockers. A fear of financial ruin, for example, can become so intense that it paralyzes action. A fear of death can destroy joy in the present. Negative thoughts of *what if* can become so intense that they block positive action. One of my patients is so afraid of cancer that the thoughts of *what if* have overwhelmed her and she refuses to allow routine lab work to be done. She claims she'd rather not know. If she ever does get cancer, she may find out about it too late to cure it, and her fear will actually have helped to produce what she fears most: death from cancer.

Whether the recordings relate to memories of the past or to fears of the present and future, a good general principle of living is to choose how to deal with the issues involved and then cut the negative thoughts and go on. Sara, the college student, needed to understand her bossiness and, above all, to change. My patient who fears cancer would feel better if she confronted her fear by getting proper medical care and then cutting the thoughts of future *what ifs*.

In the words of former President Richard Nixon:

> Worrying about things you can't do anything about is a waste of time. After I ordered the attacks on the Communist-occupied sanctuaries in Cambodia in 1970, there were violent demonstrations against my action across the nation. Some of my staff members wondered aloud whether we had made the right decision. I always put a stop to that kind of Monday morning quarterbacking by saying, "Remember Lot's wife. Don't look back." In that case I was confident I had made the right decision. But whether you are right or wrong, when you worry about the past, you cannot think about the problems you face in the present and future.[7]

Your old negative recordings block your ability to be a dream builder.

* * *

For many, a discussion over cutting these recordings becomes confused with talking about feelings or the role of faith. In other words, the recordings or mental messages that we tend to obsessively play, like *what if*, get confused with raw emotions, like fear or depression, which should not be ignored. To some, for example, emotions like fear, grief, anger, and depression indicate a lack of faith or are mistaken for a simple recording and as such are seen as negative thoughts to cut off immediately, rather than as emotions that need to be expressed and allowed to run their course.

Arising from my Christian faith and greatly influenced by my contact with those who endured the Holocaust, seeing purpose and meaning in suffering has become very important to me. My experience in an operating room years ago, during which I underwent major surgery, was very instructive to me in differentiating between recordings, feelings, and faith.

I have some potentially lethal allergies to medications. Under the best of circumstances, allergies are of concern when dealing with the powerful drugs used in connection with general anesthesia. In emergency surgery, which this was, the potential for problems becomes even greater. As the anesthesiologist inserted the intravenous tubes, he questioned me regarding some drugs, and I realized that he did not know about my allergies. There I was, in the operating room, with an IV in my arm ready to be used, explaining my allergies to the man who would choose what drugs to inject.

Once I had said all I could say to secure my safety, the recordings began to play in my mind. *What if he gives me the wrong drug and I stop breathing?* I had just published a book on medical ethics, and arising from that research, I thought, *What if I wake up on a respirator?* (This possibility happens to be a particular fear of mine.) At this point, because I had done all I could humanly do except jump off the operating table and leave, and because I had prayed about every step that I had taken, the thoughts that began to torment me were truly destructive. Nothing constructive could come from playing them. Indeed, their negative force might even have an adverse effect on how well my body handled the surgery. It was time for self talk. It was time to push the off button in my mind.

What remained were not negative recordings but feelings and faith. The feelings were those of dread, even terror. Anyone facing being knocked out by a powerful drug and then being cut open for a good two hours or more can hardly, with any sense of reason, feel happy about it. Even Christ felt great dread and agony in the Garden of Gethsemane when He faced the inevitability of the Crucifixion. I felt as if I were walking into a dark storm, but one that I had to go through in order to come out on the other side. Certainly, because of the pain I was enduring, I had no other choice.

However, overriding all of the dread was faith. That was my foundation. Prior to the excruciating pain that had sent me to the hospital, I had been reading Psalm 139 in *The Living Bible*. "You both precede and follow me, and place your hand of blessing on my head" stood out in my mind. "You ... scheduled each day of my life before I began to breathe" came back to me with simple clarity. "God was in this," I told myself. "No matter what happened to me in that operating room, God was sovereign. I would live, if that was His will. I would awake in His presence, if that was His will." The recordings dispersed. The dread was there, but paramount as I went to sleep was God's presence as a personal God. I quite literally surrendered my control directly to Him. Later I awoke in the recovery room with feelings of relief that the surgery was over and the results had been positive. I felt a deep sense of worship to God for His greatness and praise to Him for giving me more time on this earth.

In such a situation, suggesting to me that I should have no dread would have been senseless. But it was possible, even there, to cut the unnecessary recordings of *what if*. I couldn't eradicate normal feelings of fear, but I could cut the recordings, and I could make the dread bearable by focusing on God and His promises.

Sometimes we make things harder for ourselves by trying to walk on water. We expect to trust God and thereby feel no pain. We feel that because we believe in God we are exempt from pain. We pray and expect to get exactly what we want. When God says "No" to our prayers, or "Wait," we usually say that He hasn't answered our prayers. In my counseling office I see people who think that God always says "Yes" when people pray. Then, they doubt God because they feel He's let them down when He has said "No." They feel either that God isn't real or that God doesn't love them anymore. Either God has failed, or they have. It's quite a dilemma to have to choose between those two alternatives.

* * *

Not all old recordings are negative, however. Achievements in the past, tender moments with loved ones, and just plain fun times are forever stored in the granaries of our minds. They cannot be taken away; they are part of the legacy of time. In this positive area there is again a need for self talk. My work with teenage drug abusers in the late sixties and early seventies, for example, represents a time in my life that I look back on with pride. Childhood Christmases, with the relatives and the gifts and the special foods of our Swedish celebration on Christmas Eve, are a past memory that will forever give me joy. "Make a memory" is good advice for those raising children. It could aptly be changed to say "Make a recording; make a *positive* recording."

Nevertheless, sometimes past memories and achievements, even when they are positive, can be used in a destructive way in the present. Once again, all mental recordings, negative and positive, must be controlled by the habit of *cut and refocus* if dream blocking is to be avoided. It is possible to be a hero at war and never function again in normal life because the hero continues basking in the glory of the past. Just as bad childhood memories can destroy joy in the present, we can take the good memories of happy childhood times and decide that nothing in the present can ever match them.

Past joy must be savored for what it is, past joy. It must be considered a special blessing. Then, even happy memories must be cut at some point in order to focus on the present and the future. We can so live in the memories of the past or in dread of the future that the potential in the present is obliterated. Yet in reality today is tomorrow's past memory.

Used in the right way, however, positive mental recordings can help to cut the negative recordings of the present. My mother was a natural-born recording cutter. She truly knew how to turn bad times into good. Her cup was always half full. Even when she was old she went about helping the elderly, never considering herself to be one of them. When I was a child rainy days were times for home-baked goods, with all their rich aromas. Sick days were times when wonderful books were brought out to read from her seemingly endless supply. When nothing was going well, she would say, in essence, "Don't worry, it will work out," or, "God will provide." And things usually did work out, in spite of all our doubts! More amazing still, when she made these simple statements, most of us believed her, even though we didn't have the slightest idea of how anything at that point in time could possibly improve.

After the surgery I previously referred to, I thought of how my mother always turned bad times into good, and I began to look for ways to do this myself. I took past examples of how she did this, was encouraged by them, and attempted to do the same myself. Because I had had surgery in a hospital that was some distance from my home, some friends of mine had come with me and were staying in a motel by the ocean. For me, the sea itself provides memories of calmness and enablement. So after I left the hospital, I joined my friends and spent three nights recovering by the ocean, enjoying its sounds, and smelling its salty aroma, until I was well enough to travel home.

I had a choice of recordings to play. One set included *How can I afford this? What if my patients aren't doing well? When will I feel good enough to go back to work? This is a time when I wish my family were alive again.* And so the recordings could have played on, with each one yielding to a new and more disturbing one. Or, I could look at that ocean, feel its wet mist on my face, and think about the sufficiency of God who had brought me in safety to this point. I chose to play the latter recordings. It didn't just happen; I chose. Cutting the old, negative recordings was not good enough. I had to refocus, or the negative tapes would have come back. Refocusing is the key to making *cut and refocus* work.

* * *

Much of what we do with our mental recordings is automatic. By instinct, most of us play the old recordings. We hear of an earthquake across the world, and we play an instant *what if*. We remember the good old days and torture ourselves with their demise, forgetting that the good old days also had their grief.

Establishing the new pattern of *cut and refocus* means literally changing old habits and forming new ones in their place. Doing this can make the difference between heaven and hell on earth. Like all habits, old ways of dealing with these recordings die slowly, and new habits are formed by repetition. For example, if we drive home from work every night by following a certain route, we must think about changing that route or we will automatically find ourselves traveling over the old pathway once again. Only by rethinking each drive home a number of times does the new become old and thus automatic. The same is true of dealing with tapes in general until, at last, the new becomes automatic, and we find ourselves controlling those recordings, bad and good, rather than being under their control. Once the new automatic is in force, our recordings are no longer dream blockers but dream builders.

* * *

Recordings do not apply only to our personal lives. They relate to our work. Writers often refer to writer's block. In my earlier days as a writer, I always dreaded getting it. It was a kind of mysterious disease peculiar to writers, made more mysterious because I wasn't sure how you got it or how you got rid of it. Actually, a fear, a *what if* of writers block is in itself a negative recording and can cause the situation it fears. I have since found that writing is much more controllable than all of that.

To start a day of writing is to plunge into the unknown, with a hope that it goes well and never any certainty about how it will turn out. About twice a year, it just doesn't work. The writing goes badly, and it is best to stop. I suppose that in itself is some form of writer's block.

Usually, however, for me if I focus long enough on the topic, the recording of what I want to say starts. Ideas develop and illustrations come until the recording plays full force, interest peaks, and the topic becomes the most important thing in the world for that time. Yet all of this emotion and creativity starts with an act of will to play the recordings, the ideas, of whatever I am going to write about.

Perhaps because of the intensity and challenge of the recordings, I love writing days. I feel enclosed in the world of ideas in a rare, intimate communication with people I will never meet on this earth but who will, I hope, be helped by what I write. To be a writer is a rare privilege from God. To be a writer is to play recordings with a very deep and yet positive intensity.

Most work involves playing some sort of mental recording. As a teacher, I spent time focusing on the day's lesson, like a certain piece of literature or an aspect of grammar. If I didn't first get myself interested in these topics, in no way could I communicate them to my students. As a counselor, I find that each hour with each patient requires my becoming involved in the recordings of his or her life, so that for that hour the patient's problems are of primary importance to me. To lose myself in the life of another is to play a recording of that person's needs. Furthermore, to give constructive help involves an intense analysis of what can be said and done to address those needs. By use of the same principle, to cut the recordings of that patient's problems once the hour's work is completed is to preserve my own ability to go on to help the next patient and eventually to leave the counseling office and continue to build my own personal dreams.

The principle of using the mental recording theory as a tool at work holds true even in jobs that involve mechanical skills, like fixing an airplane. We all hope that an airplane mechanic focuses on the part to be fixed rather than becoming absorbed in recordings of his or her marital problems. Indeed, the ability to handle personal recordings effectively is pivotal to professionalism in almost any job.

People can work indifferently, without intense involvement, but in most jobs the results of such work are unsatisfactory. We have all been victims of teachers who hate their subject matter or, worse still, dislike their students. Many of us have known of counselors who go to sleep while their patients are talking.

Recordings are also involved, if with greater subtlety, in numerous other life activities. For example, playing recordings explains our experiences of going Christmas shopping with a resolve to cut down this year's expenses until we enter the first store. Music plays and reminds us that Christmas comes but once a year. Christmas trimmings in bright red and green, Christmas trees with colored balls and twinkling lights, Santa Claus surrounded by his elves and taking orders from wide-eyed children, people with curiously shaped bundles – all these play the mental recording of Christmas in us, and we willingly abandon our resolve to be prudent. Suddenly, nothing but Christmas seems important. January seems far away. Only when the bills arrive much later do we play once again the old-new recording of *Next year I'm going to cut down.*

* * *

People who seek counseling often feel they are weak because they have problems or, worse still, that they are weak simply because they have sought counseling. Some have even gone so far as to feel that for as long as they can hold out against seeking help they are strong. To these people, the very act of seeking help becomes an act of weakness.

Most people I see in counseling are strong. Many of them have just not learned how to use some basic, relatively simple tools in their lives. I once saw a woman who had sought the help of another professional because her marriage was falling apart and she was depressed. The advice given to Marie was to take leave from her job, stay home, and think through her depression.

By the time she saw me for the first time two weeks later, she was desperate. She had been thinking about all the depressing aspects of her life for two full weeks. She had played recordings until she was on the edge of an emotional abyss.

"Go back to work *now*" was my first piece of advice. "Then we'll build from there."

"I can't," she replied. "I'm too depressed."

The next day she went back to work. Two weeks later she sat in my office talking intelligently about some concrete solutions to her marital problems. "I can't believe how good I feel compared to two weeks ago," she commented. In truth, the results of counseling had not been that miraculous. Marie had simply cut her recordings and refocused. She had never been *weak,* whatever people mean when they use that term. She had learned some simple tools of mental health in the safety zone of a counseling office. She had cut the negative recordings that were blocking the fulfillment of her dreams. She was becoming whole. For certain people who are depressed the solution might not be this simple. But for many it is.

* * *

A great many things that happen to people in this world just happen. Years ago a friend of mine, his wife, and their three children were hit head-on by a truck driven by a drunken driver. The whole family, with the exception of one child, was killed instantly. Nothing they could have done would have prevented that accident.

Many situations can be changed, however, more than most of us realize. Perhaps one of the greatest lessons to be learned in the safety zone of counseling is that our lives can improve. We can become whole instead of fragmented because of how we handle negative recordings that play in our minds. Seemingly impossible situations can change. We each have choices to make and the power to choose lies within each human being.

What strange creatures we are! I suppose every man is a trinity, certainly every Christian man is, – spirit, soul, and body, – and we may be in three states at once, and we may not know which of the three is our real state. The whole three may be so mixed up that we become a puzzle to ourselves.

* * *

There are a great many of you who appear to have a large stock of faith, but it is only because you are in very good health and your business is prospering. If you happened to get a disordered liver, or your business should fail, I should not be surprised if nine parts out of ten of your wonderful faith should evaporate. I have noticed that certain brethren, who talk about being perfect, are generally persons of robust constitution, with a very comfortable income, and not much to do except to go about to conferences and conventions, and talk about themselves; but the tried people of God do not often ride upon those high horses. They have to cry out very frequently, and they have so many anxieties and cares which, although they cast them upon the Lord, make them realize that they are not yet pure spirits, but are still in the body. Let a man have a bad headache for about half an hour, and let him see whether he does not feel himself to be mortal.

– Charles H. Spurgeon

Four

The Body and the Mind

Mark appeared to be an average businessman. In his mid forties, he worked as a stockbroker, had three teenage girls, and enjoyed a satisfactory, if not perfect, marriage. Yet in recent days there were cracks appearing in that marriage: more arguments than usual, increased spending on the part of his wife, and some distancing by each of them. "Maybe it's just mid-life crisis," his wife had said. But Mark felt it could be more.

Sitting in my office Mark had some difficulty explaining why he was there. After going through a litany of problems Mark finally exclaimed, "Maybe I'm just depressed." When I asked how long he had felt this depression he answered nonchalantly, "All my life."

Yes, there were issues to work through; but of equal importance was a sort of gnawing depression, a gray rather than black mood, which he had felt since boyhood. Indeed he was so accustomed to it that he had almost begun to feel that it was normal. While we started to work on some practical aspects of his marital relationship, I urged him to consult a physician regarding the possibility of anti depressant medication which can sometimes help as an adjunct to therapy. At first he was resistant but then decided to try it.

In the treatment of depression it is sometimes best to combine talk therapy and medication as the ideal approach; the downside of such an approach is that at the end of treatment often you do not know how effective either would have been without the other. A way to avoid that dilemma is to start with counseling and then add medication if needed. The same principle is true in dealing with anxiety. With one young woman whom I treated for anxiety, her physician gave her a prescription for anti-anxiety medication which she carried around in her purse for security but ended up never using. Talk therapy was her real need.

With Mark, since the depression had become such an integral part of his life for so long, it seemed senseless to ignore the need for medication. No, he would not have gone out and killed himself. And, yes, solving some marital problems would help. But still the depression had been there long before he had ever met his wife. After several weeks of medication and therapy Mark began to feel the depression lessen. With a few minor adjustments of dosage the biochemical basis for his lifelong depression was sufficiently treated.

I had become used to a quiet, serious-looking man when suddenly I began to notice more facial expressions, even smiles and a gentle kind of humor. The marriage, too, was a happier one for both individuals. Medical treatment of an underlying depressive component along with some changes in both spouses' approach to some marital differences had effected a cure. More specifically, a physical component along with various psychological dimensions had worked together to bring about greater mental health.

In the treatment of human emotions, far too often the physical dimension is ignored and the problem is over-spiritualized and/or over-psychologized. At that point, since nothing else may work, the patient can be over-medicated with psychotropic drugs. Excessive amounts of medication can result in masking the contributing psychological, physical, or spiritual cause of the problem or, in the case of a wrong choice of medication or too great a combination of drugs, the patient can suffer unpleasant side effects. When medication is legitimately needed, usually a good approach is to start low and then gradually increase the dosage, or change the actual drug used, as needed.

If a person has a physical disorder like cancer it is obvious that you don't treat the actual disease with talk therapy. You treat it with surgery and/or other medical treatments. Spiritual and psychological treatment can help fortify the person who is going through physical treatment, but apart from a miracle they won't effect a cure.

Similarly, when a person presents a mainly psychological problem it should be obvious that it requires skilled psychological treatment. With psychological problems the issues are not always as clear cut as a precisely diagnosed physical disease, like cancer. For that reason, at times added physical treatment as well as spiritual help may be appropriate, sometimes on a trial and error basis. Likewise, when a person finds himself in spiritual distress the treatment may well fit into the pastoral care area altogether. But at times even then some counseling and/or medication may be a helpful adjunct.

God has made us body, mind, and spirit. Let us use these areas with care in our treatment of emotional distress. Let us be careful that we are led by principle, not pride, in our decision to use or not use psychotropic medicine or, indeed, in our determination to receive help for ourselves in any of the legitimate dimensions of body, mind, spirit.

* * *

The importance of the mind-body relationship extends way beyond the simple decision to use psychotropic medication. Relating back to Freud's prediction that someday we would find better techniques, both psychological and physical, in our treatment of mental illness, increasingly we are finding direct, often treatable, connections between mind and body. Imbalances in female hormone levels are more precisely diagnosable and treatable than they used to be; and it is commonly recognized that such imbalances can cause both anxiety and/or depression. Indeed, Postpartum Psychosis can be fatal when it ends in suicide and/or the killing of an infant. Yet there was a time when a woman in that state of psychosis was believed to be simply resentful of her newborn child. This attitude added a cruel dimension to an already painful depression. In the same way, PMS was considered to indicate resentment over growing up, in the case of adolescents, or a rebellion over being a woman when the individual was already grown up.

In another example, before conditions relating to the functioning of the thyroid gland were understood and treatable, people with related symptoms, like excessive fatigue or depression and anxiety, were labeled as lazy or, in the instance of the emotional symptoms, were told that their problems were either spiritual or that they had some kind of vague emotional problem. Then, when spiritual or psychological treatment did not work, the patient was left feeling either sinful or weak emotionally, depending on their orientation.

In this way mental illness and sin have often been the excuse for undiagnosed medical problems. If it can't be diagnosed then it must be psychological or spiritual has sometimes been the prevailing attitude. Balance is vital. It is true that sin can at times cause emotional and spiritual distress. How often do we hear of criminals who seem to get away with a crime only to be unable to keep quiet about it even years after the event? Deep down their feelings of guilt make them talk and that guilt which is based on reality eats at them. But it is important to realize also that there is such a thing as neurotic guilt which is not based on sin or reality.

In the psychological realm, too, there are problems which arise from life experiences rather than biochemical imbalances: self esteem issues from childhood, Post Traumatic Stress Syndrome from becoming a victim of a crime or from fighting in the military, school phobias from being a victim of bullying on a school yard, or a variety of symptoms resulting from abuse at any age.

Yet, once again, usually each of these various dimensions of the personality affect each other and treatment on several levels can often be the most effective approach. Just last week I had a fascinating example of the interrelationship of mind/body. A middle-aged couple who have pet lizards brought one in a cage to their joint session. They had been fighting aggressively before they saw me. At the outset of the session the lizard was brown, stick-like in appearance. At the start of our time together the couple continued the fight. Then they gradually became more reasonable and began to really listen to what the other person was saying. At the end of the counseling session they picked up the cage and I once again saw the lizard – now a bright green. As I gasped at the change, the wife commented: "Oh, he always looks like that when he's relaxed. He's just brown when he's stressed out!" I reminded them of how stressful part of the session had been and pointed out how extremely stressful their pre-session fight must have been if the lizard could relax that much in what I considered an hour filled with tension. The incident was a simple and therefore graphic example of how much emotional stress affects the body. Body, mind, spirit definitely go in both directions. The body affects the mind and the mind affects the body, and the same is true in all combinations of these three components with all of their various dimensions.

* * *

A certain level of humility is appropriate in the healing ministries – physical, psychological, and spiritual. Too often the answers are not clear or not complete. That will probably always be true, for only our Maker knows all about our inner workings in all areas. Each of us can contribute examples of how much is still not known about ourselves. For example, when I was in my early twenties I had some symptoms of fatigue, out of which eventually developed feelings of anxiety. My condition went largely undiagnosed. An unusually perceptive physician wondered if I had something called Hashimoto's, an autoimmune thyroid disorder, but there were no accurate diagnostic tests at the time. Certain laboratories did free experimental testing to help them establish a test which could work, but the results were largely futile. The doctor treated me as best he could and eventually the diagnosis was largely forgotten. The fatigue remained. Thirty years later a Rheumatologist did a battery of tests and routinely told me I had Hashimoto's! The test had finally been developed and, going by my symptoms, she had run the test.

Through the years other physical factors contributed to the symptoms. Because there was no diagnosis for so long, however, I was open to all sorts of theories and treatments. I went from various types of alternative medicine, some which made sense and some which were pure quackery, to overspiritualizing and thinking there must be some sin which I hadn't discovered yet. Finally I decided to run it by the psychological community. I ended up with a well trained, so-called secular therapist who admired my spiritual beliefs, could not find any real psychological basis for my symptoms, and stated firmly that he believed that I had some underlying physical problem which had not been properly diagnosed. I learned at least to pace myself physically, and to insulate myself from criticism relating to not doing things which pushed me beyond my physical boundaries. I also learned to walk with God in a moment by moment way, seeking His encouragement and His guidance on when to say "No." I had to realize that burning out for God was not usually God's will. I had to learn that people didn't always understand how I felt.

For me the big "breakthrough" came when at least three different physicians diagnosed me with Chronic Fatigue Syndrome, thereby validating my symptoms. At the time of this writing "cure" is not yet a word applicable to CFS and treatment for Hashimoto's has not made enough of a difference in how I feel. My experience, however, has taught me that we need to accept the unknown when we truly encounter it. Just because there's no physical diagnosis doesn't mean a problem is psychological or spiritual. Psychological and/or spiritual can become catchalls for anything we can't explain in human experience. Sometimes we just don't have the answer.

Mind/body research, however, seems to be progressing at a greater speed than ever before.

* * *

In our knowledge of the chemistry of the brain we are just beginning to see some of the implications of what Freud might have meant when he talked about other physical cures and the close relationship of body and mind. In the area of brain chemistry, for example, the brain used to be conceived as predetermined almost entirely by the genes, basically unchangeable by human will or environment past early childhood. Now, however, thanks to brain imaging and because of more recent research, we know that the brain possesses great neuroplasticity.

Just by case studies life itself should have given us a clue before this time. For example, the famous scientist Louis Pasteur suffered a major stroke in 1868. At forty-five he was already a prominent French scientist and had invented the pasteurization process. Yet it was after a major stroke and continuing small ones that he recovered enough to perform his greatest scientific feats, including the development of a Rabies vaccine. Brain cells obviously adapted enough to perform new functions. According to researcher Jeffrey Schwartz, MD, the will can actually change the brain in conditions like OCD (Obsessive Compulsive Disorder) and stroke. The way we think can cause plastic changes in the brain.[1] Furthermore, neurogenesis, the development of new neurons, a process which has previously been considered impossible, is now a fact of neuroscience. Pasteur had more going for him than anyone realized.

In my own practice, particularly in the use of *cut and refocus*, I have seen some dramatic results which I now realize relate in part to brain chemistry. One example concerned a strikingly attractive, bright actress in her mid thirties who consulted me a number of years ago for ongoing depression. For the most part the intensity of Christine's depression was relatively mild. Yet whenever a crisis arose she resorted to a suicide attempt. This had started way back in her teens and had become an automatic response to stress. "She didn't want to die that much," you might say, and yet after one attempt she was on life support for a month until she suddenly awakened from her coma. She had been to a variety of psychiatrists, psychologists, and pastors before I met her. As we talked I realized that while she did not appear to be deeply depressed, and even seemed to have a joy of life, suicide had become a sort of bad habit, albeit a dangerous one.

"I can't stop you from killing yourself," I told her as I established some boundaries. "And if you do attempt it again you'll need 911, not me." Previous therapists had brought flowers to the hospital and reinforced her sense of victimization from her bad past. At the risk of sounding cold I did not want to affirm this rather bizarre habit she had developed in response to everyday stress, like a fight with her husband.

Her whole view of herself began to improve. Gradually she substituted breaking dishes for suicide. Her husband, understandably relieved, gratefully replaced the expensive china until I intervened. Christine agreed with that decision and worked out healthier and less expensive ways of dealing with frustration.

Still we were on new ground now and I didn't totally believe that the old recordings of suicidal impulses would not come back at least once. It felt a little like I was watching an alcoholic refuse drinks for a year, hoping the pattern lasted. Only in Christine's case the stakes were higher and more final.

At the end of each session I reminded her that if she was ever tempted to try suicide again she needed to remember that she didn't have to. There were other choices. It was a matter of choice – her choice. Dismissively she would tell me that I didn't have to remind her, she knew that. But she tolerated my three-minute intrusion into her hour.

I was out of town when it happened. There were several phone calls from her husband who never did call 911 or anyone else. He just left messages like, "Where are you when we need you!" Then at the end of the messages there was a calm call from Christine, "Would you call me when you get back?"

"I'm so glad you weren't here," she said when I first talked to her. Then she explained. She had been over-medicated during a minor outpatient surgery. Upon arriving home she became angry over a small incident. Then her old automatics came into play. She grabbed a knife, went into the bathroom and told her husband she was going to kill herself. He raced off to call me – hence the messages. While he was phoning, Christine suddenly stopped and exclaimed out loud: "Elizabeth's right. I don't have to do this. I can choose." Then she went into her bedroom and slept off the drugs.

In that first phone conversation with me she exclaimed: "It's the first time in my life that my emotions haven't controlled me. I controlled them." For ten years until her death from a heart condition she never again attempted suicide.

* * *

The brain has always been a source of much speculation and little knowledge. However, brain research is now becoming more extensive. In a vast oversimplification of how this research applies in this book, we know that the brain has two general functions: the *mechanical brain* which controls bodily functions and the *mind* which is the center of thinking. It is the mind with which we are concerned when we think about behavioral change. Brain cells are called neurons, although that term also applies to all nerve cells. These neurons (of which there are about one hundred billion) communicate with each other across open spaces between them called *synapses*. They do this by creating chemical explosions. This activity is similar to electricity. The "messages" are ultimately blasted from a neuron through molecules in the neuron which are called *neurotransmitters*. In that way information is sent.

Toward the center of the brain there are two main areas of interest in connection with the focus of this book: the *amygdala*, which is the emotional processor of the brain and perhaps helps in the selection of long-term memories by determining their emotional significance, and the *hippocampus*, often considered the primary memory system, which decides whether information and experiences which the brain processes are stored as short term memory or long term. For example, the toast I ate for breakfast this morning is not likely to be remembered next week or perhaps even tomorrow. Yet I still remember the first time I used a "finger bowl" as a child at the St. Frances Hotel in San Francisco. It was a new experience, it was a fancy restaurant, we were on vacation, and the waiter regaled us with stories of when my childhood hero, General Douglas MacArthur, had eaten there. In short there was a heavy focus on the event, unlike the memory of my routine toast, and so the hippocampus interpreted the memory as important and therefore worthy of long-term memory.

In a very interesting documentary on the brain the story was told of a man who was picked up wandering, confused, and lost on a city street. He gave an age which was eleven years younger than what he turned out to be. He said his wife was pregnant, whereas in fact the child had been born eleven years previous. He gave an address which was also eleven years back. When he was examined a cyst was discovered which cut off access to the Hippocampus. When the cyst was removed eleven years of memories flooded back. Such is the remarkable quality of the brain.[2]

* * *

Even more remarkably, it has now been proved that not only does the brain have plasticity but, as previously shown, new neurons can form. Also neurons can adapt to new functions, as in the case of Pasteur. They simply change jobs. It has long been common knowledge that persons who lose their sight seem to develop extra ability in other senses, like hearing and touch. There is evidence now that neurons which respond to commands from the visual cortex no longer receive messages relating to sight after blindness occurs. Over time these neurons change their function and reinforce activity in the other senses.

In the example of Christine, as she recognized that *she* could control these suicidal impulses, the neurotransmitters which had been previously trained to signal a suicidal impulse, she *did* control them by *cut* – "I don't have to follow that impulse" – and *refocus* – "I will now attend to something that keeps my interest." After repeated times the change in pattern apparently changed the activity of the neurotransmitters and built new automatics.

* * *

It is because of the plasticity of the brain that these exercises of cognitive behavioral therapy can be of help. Michael Merzenich, M.D., back as early as the late sixties, did some important, groundbreaking research in this area and surprised even himself when he concluded, "The brain had to be plastic."[3] Dr. Jeffrey Schwartz, M.D., a research professor of psychiatry at the UCLA School of Medicine has done some remarkable research on brain plasticity, particularly as it relates to OCD (Obsessive Compulsive Disorder). In essence he claims that the brain can relearn and establish new automatics. For this he has established a four-step plan of basically self help.

Understanding this research as explained in his book *The Mind and the Brain*, co-authored with Sharon Begley, has helped me comprehend more completely my *cut and refocus* approach. For example, with a patient who obsesses a *what if* of the future, *cut* – as in turn off the recording – becomes more specific in meaning. Identify the *what if* as a messed up neuron, a mixed up message and realize "I'm not required to give it credence. It's just my neurons firing off the wrong electrical impulses." More importantly, after *cut* comes *refocus*.

* * *

In addition to psychotherapeutic techniques, and especially with the proliferation of new psychotropic drugs, medication has brought added relief to many people. The selective serotonin reuptake inhibitors (SSRIs) are less risky than some of the original psychotropic drugs used to treat conditions involving depression and anxiety. Serotonin, a neurotransmitter, is connected with feelings of well being. These SSRI drugs lengthen the amount of time that the serotonin persists in the synapse because the uptake mechanism which normally removes it has been blocked by the drug. Prozac is one of the earliest and most popular of these drugs. Serotonin levels are also enhanced by sunlight, a fact which may in part account for high suicide rates in geographical locations like northern Sweden, where sunlight is very limited at certain times of the year. This condition is called Seasonal Affective Disorder or SAD.

Some clinical trials have indicated that medication combined with psychotherapy can be the most effective treatment. There are too many variables to state emphatically what works best for any given individual with his or her unique problems. But this is where it is essential that any individual in need of help seeks information from reliable sources in order to find the best treatment for them.

Dr. Schwartz offers a valid warning regarding what he calls using "mental force" or the "direct action of mind on brain":

> An obvious question is how far one can extend
> the reach of the hypothesized mental force. As

the Decade of the Brain ended, neuroscientists had mapped out the neural circuits that underlie myriad states and behaviors, from depression to aggression to suicidal impulses. Does the existence of mental force imply that with enough attention and volition the violent teen can will himself the brain circuits that make a civilized adult of him? That the suicidal widow can will herself the neural circuits correlated with a love of life, or at least spiritual acceptance? That the schizophrenic can will his voices to be silent, and his visions to disappear? The power of cognitive-behavioral therapy to alter brain circuits in people with either depression or OCD implies that similar therapy, drawing on mental force, should be able to change other circuitry that underlies an aspect of personality, behavior, even thought. And that, of course, encompasses approximately everything, from the mundane to the profound: addiction or temperance, a bad temper or a forgiving nature, impatience or patience, love of learning or antipathy to it, generosity or niggardliness, prejudice or tolerance.

There is a danger to this way of thinking: it treads close to the position that anyone with a mental illness remains sick because of a failure of will, anyone with an undesirable personality trait retains it because she has failed to exert sufficient mental effort. Even those of us who distrust the "My genes (or my neurochemicals) made me do it" school of human behavior back

> away from the implication that will alone can
> bring into being the neural circuitry capable
> of supporting any temperament or behavioral
> tendency – indeed, any state of mental health.
> But to frame the issue in this all-or-nothing way
> is to create a simplistic, and false, choice.[4]

Yet "The life we lead, in other words, leaves its mark in the enduring changes in the complex circuitry of the brain – footprints of the experiences we have had, the actions we have taken. This is neuroplasticity."[5]

Ultimately, for those of us who value our faith in Someone beyond ourselves, a divine Being, the following conclusion is affirming: "The teachings of faith have long railed against the perils of the materialist mind-set. Now neuroscience and physics have joined them at the barricades. The science emerging with the new century tells us that we are not the children of matter alone, nor its slaves."[6]

The resources of the body/mind treatments can be liberating for so many of the problems which we human beings find ourselves enduring and trying to cure. To watch that "cure" happen is one of the greatest joys of dealing with the emotional problems of human beings.

* * *

Above all of this, but not in contradiction to it, not only can a relationship with God be a help or even a cure, it is this spiritual dimension which ultimately can be depended upon. As human will has its place in shaping the direction of the brain, so human will relates to how much God is allowed to intervene. For as one old saint once said, Jesus Christ is always a gentleman. He will not intrude where He is not wanted.

In this connection, now that we understand the plasticity of the brain it behooves us to watch what we expose our minds to. The poet John Milton once wrote:

> The mind is its own place, and in it self
> Can make a Heav'n of Hell, a Hell of
> Heav'n.[7]

To quote another researcher, Paula Tallal of Rutgers University: "'You create your brain from the input you get.'"[8]

Music, for example, is a very important factor in long-term memory. There is strong evidence that listening to certain kinds of music, like Mozart, can enhance certain types of intellectual functioning. What kind of music do we listen to? What serious evaluation is going into the choice of the music we sing in our church services? Repetition is important also in what the brain retains, but having said that there is no positive justification for the mindless, irreverent, hypnotic so-called worship music which seems to be prevalent in so many church services.

What about scriptural memorization? God who made our brain knows how what we learn affects our behavior and thus we are admonished to hide God's word in our hearts (Psalm 119:11). What about our everyday thinking and talking? In Philippians 4:8 we are told what our mind should be focused on: "...whatsoever things are true, whatsoever things are honest, whatsoever things are just, whatsoever things are pure, whatsoever things are lovely, whatsoever things are of good report; if there be any virtue, and if there be any praise, think on these things." According to Bible translator and expositor Kenneth Wuest, "The word 'think' in the Greek speaks of the act of careful reflection."[9] With the power of the Internet and with the choices we are offered on TV and in the theater, we need to be aware of how much we determine the quality of our thinking by our input and even by the changes which occur in our brain by our use of the electronic media. For a constant input of evil into our brain can well account for something of the meaning of I Timothy 4:2 when he speaks of a "conscience seared with a hot iron."

* * *

There is ample anecdotal evidence reinforced by findings within the scientific community that brain patterns are significantly influenced by cultural factors like television and the Internet. According to Dr. Merzenich:

> The Internet is just one of those things that contemporary humans can spend millions of "practice" events at, that the average human a thousand years ago had absolutely no exposure to. Our brains are massively remodeled by this exposure – but so, too, by reading, by television, by video games, by modern electronics, by contemporary music, by contemporary "tools," etc.[10]

While most of us are concerned with media content, i.e. violence, we fail to factor in the enormous impact of the medium itself.

In a study of twenty-six hundred toddlers, it was shown that children between the ages of one and three who watch television are more inclined to have problems with their attention span and impulse control in later years. "For every hour of TV the toddlers watched each day, their chances of developing serious attentional difficulties at age seven increased by 10 percent."

Harvard psychiatrist Edward Hallowell, an expert on ADD (Attention Deficit Disorder), connects the rising incidence of ADD, when it is not genetically produced, to the increased use of electronic media.[11]

Not long ago I went to see a movie which was child appropriate and not as fast moving as the average movie today. What amazed me were the trailers for movies, presumably labeled as child appropriate. There were constant abrupt acts of violence, like cars crashing and airplanes falling. The noise was loud and everything was fast and unpredictable. What this does in a practical sense is cause an heightened need for "high speed transitions in the media." This need produces difficulty in focus. Increasingly education has to be doled out in small increments and even some college classes are reportedly "dumbed down."

Supporting this view of actual brain changes:

> A team at the Hammersmith Hospital in London designed a typical video game in which a tank commander shoots the enemy and dodges enemy fire. The experiment showed that dopamine – the reward neurotransmitter, also triggered by addictive drugs – is released in the brain during these games. People who are addicted to computer games show all the signs of other addictions: cravings when they stop, neglect of other activities, euphoria when on the computer, and a tendency to deny or minimize their actual involvement.[12]

* * *

Other factors affect brain wellness. Refined carbohydrates, causing imbalances in sugar and insulin levels in the body, added to excessive stress or a sedentary lifestyle, can be detrimental to brain function. In short, many factors which harm the cardiovascular system are also detrimental to brain fitness. The Alzheimer's Association recommends a diet high in antioxidants: dark colored vegetables like spinach and beets and bright colored fruits like berries, raisins, oranges, and red grapes. They also add foods high in Omega-3 fatty acids, like salmon or trout.[13] Combine some of the mental training programs which are now available to a brisk session of physical exercise along with good socialization and you have a brain which is more likely to be functioning at its optimal level.

Exercise in particular seems to play a unique part in brain plasticity and neurogenesis. John J. Ratey, M.D., makes the point clearly in his book *Spark: The Revolutionary New Science of Exercise and the Brain.*

> In October of 2000 researchers from Duke University made the *New York Times* with a study showing that exercise is better than sertraline (Zoloft) at treating depression. What great news! Unfortunately, it was buried on page fourteen of the Health and Fitness section. If exercise came in pill form, it would be plastered across the front page, hailed as the blockbuster drug of the century.[14]

Actually at the time of this writing the exercise pill has become a reality which did appear recently all over the media. I have included this quotation, however, in order to emphasize the importance of exercise. But once again, balance is essential. Some people need psychotropic medication, so don't throw away your Zoloft yet. We are each unique human beings with different biochemical makeup. For some, exercise may do the job. But I would be willing to guess that medication, nutrition, exercise, talk therapy, and other treatments often combine to obtain the best results. Furthermore, brain research of any depth is new and will undoubtedly change and improve with time. Ultimately, however, only God will totally understand this remarkable organ which He has created.

* * *

The new-old exciting fact is that we no longer need to view ourselves as the predetermined victims or even robots of a brain which is permanently mapped out without our input or the possibility of change. Years ago a businessman in his forties came to me at his wife's insistence. The man was just starting to think that people might be out to get him, even to the level of actually poisoning his doorknobs. I decided to see him briefly as I worked toward making him willing to seek more specialized help.

First I made it clear that I believed him, his truthfulness, but made it equally clear that I did not believe that he was in physical danger. I did not believe he was lying, but I did feel that his perception of the truth was inaccurate. No doorknobs were poisoned! He listened and did not seem offended. I kept urging him to ignore, not to place credence in, the idea of poisoned doorknobs – indeed to act opposite to what his emotions were telling him. At first he politely went on with his earlier convictions that someone was out to get him. Then the thoughts vanished.

He was no longer tortured by his fears. He could perceive reality once again. According to occasional updates which I got from his wife for several years after I last saw him I learned that the results had lasted. In view of what we now know about the plasticity of the brain I now believe that his brain chemistry actually changed.

* * *

In an even more amazing example of how brain cells literally change jobs and adapt to new functions, Dr. Ratey tells the story of an 85-year-old nun:

> There was a nun named Sister Bernadette who died of a heart attack at age eighty-five in the mid-1990s. Along with more than six hundred other nuns, she donated her brain to science as part of an ongoing study conducted by epidemiologist

David Snowdon, who memorialized the School Sisters of Notre Dame, in Mankato, Minnesota, in his inspiring book, *Aging with Grace*. The nuns constantly challenge their minds, with vocabulary quizzes, mental puzzles, and debates about public issues, and many of them live to be one hundred or more. The interesting thing about Sister Bernadette is that she scored in the ninetieth percentile on cognitive tests right up until she died, but when her brain was examined postmortem, it showed massive damage from Alzheimer's disease. Tissue from her hippocampus to her cortex was riddled with plaque and neurofibrillary tangles to the most extensive degree, and she also carried the ApoE4 gene variant. In other words, she should have been utterly lost to the ravages of dementia. Yet despite the damage in her brain, she remained mentally sharp.

...By teaching until a late age and staying mentally active, Sister Bernadette almost certainly trained her brain to work around the genetic hand she was dealt.[15]

* * *

The miraculous working together of the body, mind, and spirit is ultimately eclipsed, however, as we recognize the power of God Himself.

A few days after lengthy and serious abdominal surgery I was recovering well but was still groggy from the drugs and weak from the trauma of what my body had come through. Once again, one of my greatest fears going into surgery had been the threat of an allergic reaction to the medications involved. Having experienced anaphylactic shock more than once to drugs like penicillin, I knew that certain chemicals had the potential to create fatal reactions.

Now as I lay on my hospital bed I felt relief that the worst was over. I had done well with the anesthesia, and even the severe infection had been treated safely in spite of the massive amount of drugs needed.

A nurse walked in at that point of my ruminations. "I have a new drug for your IV," she said cheerfully. A sudden sense of alert hit me. "You need to check the inactive ingredients," I said. "Make sure there are no parabens."

"I'm sure it's fine," she said soothingly. A resident who had entered the room concurred with her on that point. Remembering a time when I had experienced anaphylactic shock (a severe allergic reaction) and stopped breathing from a much smaller dose of parabens (which are a common preservative), I insisted that they check for the presence of parabens in this particular medication. Somewhat irritated, but tolerant, the nurse and resident doctor left the room, medication in hand.

A few hours later the resident came back, then the charge nurse, both to thank me for refusing to take the drug until it was checked. Yes, it did have parabens!

Later when I asked more questions about what had triggered my anxiety about the drug, I was told that there was no incident which had caused me to be alarmed – nothing but a quiet, persistent divine urging to stop. To use the vernacular it was a "God thing." I had come through excellent treatment in one of the top medical centers in the country. Yet one oversight involving one drug out of many could have caused death. But – then there was God. As integrated as we are and as multidimensional the treatment for any aspect of medical or behavioral care, above it all there is God.

In circles where self-contempt is preached, it is of course never explained why a person should be so ill-mannered and inconsiderate as to force his company on other people if he finds it so dreary and deadening himself. And furthermore the multitude of contradictions are never adequately explained in a doctrine which advises that we should hate the one self, "I," and love all others with the obvious expectation that they will love us, hateful creatures that we are; or that the more we hate ourselves, the more we love God who made the mistake, in an off moment, of creating this contemptible creature, "I."

– Dr. Rollo May

FIVE

DREAM BLOCKS

When I was a high school English teacher, a favorite composition topic that I used to assign to my classes was: "If you could be anything in the whole world, without regard to practical factors, like money, time, preparation, and ability, what would you choose to become?" After my students had taken time to think and write down their dreams, we talked about how some of these dreams might come true.

For example, maybe that student from a poor family, who wanted to be a doctor but couldn't afford medical school, could apply for a scholarship. Perhaps the girl who wanted to be a hairstylist but was taking college preparatory classes in order to please her parents should talk to them more directly about her goals and then change to cosmetology. Maybe that boy who wished he were smart enough to be a veterinarian should discover all the related jobs that don't require as much training instead of giving up on working with animals altogether.

Ten years later, as a beginning writer I found myself in the same rut as these students. I hoped someone would want to publish me. Anyone! I found myself thinking that because of my lack of experience as a writer I could approach only lesser-known publishers.

Then one day I remembered those discussions with my students. "Try for the top," I used to say. "You might make it. And if you don't you've lost nothing. All they can say is no."

I found the name of an editor at one of the most respected publishing companies in the country, picked up the phone, and called. By some miracle I got this person immediately. I told her about my book idea and, to my surprise, she said she was interested. Then came the stall, the alert to me that this approach might not work after all. "Send us an outline," she said.

I'll never hear from them again, I thought. I should have stuck with unknowns.

Teachers since grammar school had been giving me a similar command: "Do an outline; then write your essay." However, I never did outlines. I was the student who wrote the essay, then did the outline, and then turned both of them in, with the teacher never realizing which was done first.

Because the project appeared doomed to failure anyway, I wrote just a one-page summary of the ideas I wanted to expand in my book and mailed it to the editor with little thought of hearing from her again. No positive thinking here! To my surprise, I got a fast answer of acceptance. The publisher actually wanted me.

In my own life I had validated what I had taught my students earlier. "Reach for your dreams and sometimes you realize them. Fail to reach, and you'll never know what you could have done."

* * *

To become a dream builder requires a certain basic amount of self-esteem. A good self-image provides much of the raw material for the building blocks with which dreams are built. A good self-image is another dimension of the total personality and wholeness. The dream of building great bridges or organizing large armies or performing delicate surgery; the dream of reaching people through the ideas written on the pages of a book or spoken with power over the airwaves; the dream of a successful marriage and children who are raised with the nurturing of Christian principles – all these are dreams that take form, in part, because of the sturdy self-esteem that enables them.

The process of developing a positive self image which helps in fulfilling dreams often starts way back in early childhood. Sometimes it begins with the motivation of a very specific childhood dream. At other times it evolves gradually, step by step as the child receives encouragement from a teacher, challenge from a parent, or counsel from a youth pastor. Ideally the growing child not only develops and reaches for dreams but at the same time builds the confidence that will help him or her actually build these dreams.

It is certainly possible to have a low self-image and still be a dream builder, but reaching for the sky is harder when you barely have enough confidence just to survive. Should you actually become a dream builder, maintaining those dreams is harder. The first flash of disapproval or failure can be enough to stop the dream building altogether.

An example of dream building that often comes to my mind is that of the great founder of the China Inland Mission (now called Overseas Missionary Fellowship). In his early years in China, Hudson Taylor buried his wife and several children in Chinese soil and received severe criticism from both the secular and religious worlds for his insistence on establishing an indigenous church in China. He was ridiculed and resented for adapting to Chinese customs of dress and social behavior rather than forcing the Chinese Christians to conform to British customs. These positions received much praise from future generations, but at the time he stood virtually alone.

Dr. Taylor had a dream of opening up the interior of China to the message of Jesus Christ. He was a dream builder. When those dreams, along with his own personal life, seemed to be crashing down around him, he had enough conviction and confidence to go on. Above all, he still believed that the God who had started him on this path would not forsake him.

Others who were not dream builders might have sunk in a mire of doubt. "Maybe this wasn't of God after all," they might reason. "Perhaps I have sinned and God has forsaken me." "God must have another person for the job." "How can I go on when even my Christian brethren do not support me?" Hudson Taylor dared to believe in his God-inspired dream and leaned harder on God with results that can be assessed only in eternity. We know even now, however, that because of a handful of missionaries like him, when Communism took over China in the late forties, Christianity did not die. It grew under the tutelage of adversity.

* * *

Most of us are not heroes. Most of us do not aspire to international or even national greatness. However, it is important for all of us to develop and maintain a level of self-esteem that can handle risk taking. In this way we will sometimes attempt the impossible and find that it is indeed very possible. On a more everyday basis, it is important to maintain a certain level of self-esteem just to perform the duties of life.

In spite of their diversity, many of the problems people bring to a counseling office such as mine are based in deficiencies in self-image. Low self-esteem manifests itself in many ways. Bragging is one symptom of a low self-image. If I don't like myself, I may keep telling you how great I am just so that I myself will be convinced. Arrogance is not good self-esteem; it arises from low self-esteem.

Self-denigration is the other extreme. Statements like "I can't do anything right" and "I'm sure they won't like me" are obvious declarations of a low self-image. A sloppy house or careless personal hygiene, as well as overfastidiousness about makeup or clothing or any perfectionism drawn to the extreme, can characterize a person who is down on himself.

More often than not, a person with a low self-image mixes this viewpoint into various aspects of his or her life. There may be insecurity about work but not about relationships. People may be uncomfortable about their appearance but not about their gardens. Some transfer their self-doubt to God and feel that even God can't stand them; others will feel that only God *does* care about them and doubt that anyone else does. Most of us may seem to have pockets of low self-esteem and pockets of high self-esteem. The symptoms vary from person to person. In the assessment of self-image, therefore, looking at the whole person is important.

"I don't even go to the doctor anymore," Sam concluded at the end of our first counseling session. "My whole family has died of cancer, and I don't want to know when I get it."

Sam was the proverbial ostrich. In his place of employment he made less money than anyone else because he couldn't bring himself to ask for a raise. Yet when extra time or skill was needed, everyone turned to Sam, who because of his desire to be liked, willingly obliged.

As a child Sam had been unfavorably compared to his older brother. "Why can't you be more like your brother?" was a favorite remark of his mother; his father called him "Stupid Sam" when he fell clumsily over his own feet or got a low grade at school.

In later years, even from his deathbed, Sam's father showed his favoritism for Sam's brother. Sam had been at his father's bedside night and day for several days without any show of gratitude from his father for his faithfulness. When Sam's brother cut a lavish vacation short by one day and finally appeared at the hospital, the father gave his older son a warm smile of greeting and said, "I knew you'd come. You always do when I need you."

Actually Sam was a bright, talented young man who, understandably, didn't even know it. "Stupid Sam" stood out in his memory as the only authoritative statement on his life. Only when it was quite obvious that his whole world was using him, and the pain got great enough, did it occur to him that he should get professional help. Through one small glimmer at a time, Sam is beginning to see that he is a sensitive, talented man whom God put on this earth for a specific purpose.

* * *

Frequently, a self-image problem is involved even when the presenting symptoms belie the fact. For as long as I have known her, Karen, a woman in her late forties, has been a perpetual victim. Beneath her tendency to feel victimized is a strong sense of inadequacy. In her mind her stepmother resented her; her natural father chose the stepmother over her and thus betrayed her; she has been neglected by her husband; and her boss abuses her willingness to work. Her emotional life cycle resembles a psychological tumbleweed, rolling in the desert sand and picking up more and more dust as it rolls along.

Realistically, Karen has had her share of genuine victimization, particularly as a child. For the most part now, however, she perceives rejection where it doesn't exist. Long ago she disliked herself so intensely that she assumed everyone else disliked her as well. She anticipated rejection where it didn't exist. She became prickly and defensive, so other people reacted in kind, only confirming to her that indeed she was unlikable. Rather than appearing to be vulnerable and insecure, as she truly was, she seemed formidable, even ruthless. Over the years she has convinced herself that she has had a rotten chance at life, and it never seems to occur to her that if *she* changed, her whole world would be different.

However, just as not everyone is like Sam in his determination to face his problems and change, not everyone is like Karen in her determination to blame her environment and to insist that if those around her would just change she could be happy. In her mind *she* doesn't have a problem; *they* do. Some people *do* know that their self-image problems are hurting their lives, but still they resist the changes in their lives that would be required for them to develop better self-images. They have grown used to hating themselves.

* * *

An older couple sat in my office and told of their severe health problems, which their doctor attributed to stress. Moving two adult children, and their spouses, three grandchildren, and one dog into their four-bedroom home with them, so that their children could save money to buy houses, had caused John to leave a thriving law practice and Marie to seek counseling. Yet what they really were seeking was some miracle answer on how it could all work. "Help us walk on water so we can do all this" was what they wanted from counseling. They did not want to face the insecurity that was driving them to help these adult children they were afraid of losing. They did not want to change. They have dreams that are buried deep inside of them, some of which they have never shared even with each other. But the dream blocks of self-esteem were broken and smashed many years ago. They are no longer dream builders; they just survive, barely.

Some people, however, want to change their lives badly enough to pay the price tag of personal growth. Charlene was a woman in her thirties who came to her first counseling session acutely aware of her self-image problems. "I like helping people," she explained, "but then when their demands increase I just can't say 'No,' and so I feel used. I need to learn to say 'No' regardless of my fear of not being considered nice." Charlene, Sam, and others like them change their lives because they decide to do so, and in so doing they become free to build their dreams, not from something ethereal and unreal but from something based in reality.

* * *

Self-esteem is a very vague and often misunderstood term; still it is a pervasive and yet fluctuating factor in every one of our lives. It affects our ability to declare our boundaries and live lives of balance. It influences how effectively we cut all negative recordings. It can make or break our ability to fulfill our God-given dreams. To some it implies a bullish sort of self-worship or arrogance. To others it sounds appealing but unattainable. Still others view good self-esteem as antithetical to faith in God. Yet for those of us in the Judeo-Christian tradition nothing is further from the truth.

The Book of Proverbs balances the issue with perfection: "A man who assists a thief must really *hate himself*! ..." Compliance in a crime leads only to greater problems; therefore a person with self-respect would not be easily drawn into the self-destructive behavior of a thief. The Book of Proverbs goes on to say: "... to *trust* in God means safety" (Prov. 29:24-25 TLB). If self-hate leads only to destruction, the obvious conclusion here is that self-acceptance is a positive dimension of good living. Combined with trust in God, it is undefeatable. We must conclude, therefore, that a good self-image is one of the positive building blocks of our human personality, building blocks God uses as long as we remember that both the building blocks and the power to use them are ultimately from Him, not of us.

In the timeless manner in which the Bible is written, a verse in the Book of Romans gives us what I consider the best definition of self-esteem: "... not to be thinking more highly of one's self, beyond that which one ought necessarily to be thinking, but to be thinking with a view to a sensible appraisal (of one's self) according as to each one God divided a measure of faith" (Rom. 12:3, Wuest). Theologian Kenneth Wuest further explains: "All of which goes to say that a Christian should appraise the gifts God has given him fairly, glorifying God for their bestowal, and their exercise through dependence upon the Holy Spirit, and not in mock humility make light of them."[1]

* * *

It is a paradox of Christianity that whereas man is in himself totally depraved and cut off from God, in Christ that same man is redeemed and endowed with God-given gifts. Cambridge scholar C. S. Lewis rightly states:

> There are no ordinary people. You have never talked to a mere mortal. Nations, cultures, arts, civilization – these are mortal, and their life is to ours as the life of a gnat. But it is immortals whom we joke with, work with, marry, snub, and exploit – immortal horrors or everlasting splendours.... Next to the Blessed Sacrament itself, your neighbor is the holiest object presented to your senses. If he is your Christian neighbor he is holy in almost the same way, for in him also Christ *vere latitat* – the glorifier and the glorified, Glory Himself, is truly hidden.[2]

In the light of God's great value of each human being, we cannot with any sanction from the teachings of Christianity decide that self-hate is Christian. For those who find that conversion to Christ is, in the words of my friend, the late British Bible scholar A. J. Crick, "the moment when I decided that God's will must be mine and I slipped into that wonderful sphere," an honest evaluation of God-given talents and gifts becomes essential as a starting point in going on to develop and maintain a good self-image. Then, change and growth are in order where sin and imperfection have marred that original perfection that was of God.

It is important, too, to recognize the difference between the vertical and horizontal views of a person's worth.

•

•

•   Man's relationship to God

•

•

•   •   •   •   •   •   •

Man's relationship to man

An indisputable Christian teaching is that compared to God, man is totally depraved, cut off from God, and in need of redemption, a redemption that is to be found in a personal acceptance of Jesus Christ. Yet God has given great talents, gifts, and qualities of personality for which every person can feel worth. These are dream blocks with which we can each build dreams.

Listening to a sermon preached by my former pastor, the late John Whorrall, I heard a quotation from Phillips Brooks that helped clarify a balanced Christian position on the whole issue of self-esteem: "The true way to be humble is not to stoop until you are smaller than yourself, but to stand at your real height against some higher nature that will show you what the real smallness of your greatness is." In our misguided efforts to be humble we sometimes try to stoop rather than to stand at our real height and grow still higher. We need not fear good self-esteem. God will always be so much higher than we are that knowing that will keep us truly humble.

* * *

Just as there is nothing unchristian about a good self-image, there is nothing unchristian about competition. The image of running a race or seeking a prize is a totally biblical concept. If I have a good grasp of intellectual issues, play the piano well, or am a good mother, I can be proud of these qualities. I can further promote my feelings of self-worth by winning a scholarship, entering a painting competition, or enjoying the fact that my children behave better in a restaurant than some others I see. If I have a truly good self-image, I won't need to gloat about these experiences; I'll just enjoy them.

Moreover, the fact that what good qualities we have are gifts from God should not diminish their importance to our sense of self-worth. When I was a small child, my parents gave me a white fur muff and a matching fur hairband for Christmas. The next Sunday morning I went to Sunday school wearing them and feeling very proud indeed. I didn't flaunt them at my friends; I just felt proud of how I looked. They weren't picked out by me, but by my mother; they weren't paid for by me, but by my father. Yet I felt proud because they were now mine. So it is with God's gifts to us. We can be proud of them because He gave them to us, and they are now ours to use in building our lives for His purposes.

Sometimes, however, our dream blocks are marred and crushed. When people cannot see positive qualities in themselves, even when others point them out, counseling can be a safety zone into which they can retreat in order to learn to view themselves more honestly. When people have talents and potentials of which they are aware and yet those abilities lie unused or are used in destructive ways, counseling can help those people develop a better self-image by helping them improve their behavior in those areas.

Thus, growth in the area of self-esteem is two-pronged: recognition of positive God-given talents, gifts, and characteristics, and behavioral change in those areas of life that are negative and not worthy of respect. For example, an intelligent student who thinks he is stupid and who fails all his classes may not succeed until he first sees his potential and then works in order to bring his performance up to that potential. Others know they are bright but need simply to study in order to succeed. The first is strictly a self-image problem; the second is a lack of self-discipline that results in low performance and causes a low self-image.

At times a person who is intellectually capable may not only neglect using that ability for positive purposes, like studying in school, but also compensate for the resultant low self-image by using that same ability for wrongdoing, such as computer theft or vandalism. In summary, to have a good self-image, some people need to see their worth; others need to behave in a more worthwhile way. Both are important dimensions of our psychological makeup.

* * *

Pride is the counterfeit of good self-esteem, and what Kenneth Wuest calls "mock humility" is simply an unchristian condition of self-hate. Either pride or mock humility indicates a sense of low self-esteem and defective dream blocks that make dream building ineffective or even impossible. The Christian teaching that condemns pride and advocates humility can be understood only by a correct definition of these terms, an understanding that is also a basis for good mental health.

To admit to problems of low self-esteem offends the pride of some people. In a paradoxical way, if we truly do not like ourselves, it is hard to have enough self-confidence to admit to fault. A bluff of "I'm the greatest" or the development of a dictatorial personality may be a cover for the truth, which is "I don't like myself." Periodically I see men who accept the biblical injunction to be heads of their families and forget that they are commanded by the same Bible to love their wives as they love their own bodies. The result is a harsh, dictatorial attitude. They do not have too much ego but too little. Archaic as it may seem, in my years of counseling I have seen more than one man who felt that some form of spousal abuse was a form of godly discipline for which he was responsible. I have counseled men who make unreasonable sexual demands and wives who submit because they think it is the Christian way.

Yet within the marriage relationship, men are not always arrogant in their manifestation of low self-esteem. Often it shows itself in a false humility, a sort of groveling. I can think of one man who values the corner of his garage as his only refuge. For years a dominating wife has degraded him in front of their children and demeaned him before his friends. He has learned that to fight back only makes it worse, so he retreats. In her self-hate, his wife lashes out. Because he does not value himself, he withdraws. Through the years their reactions to each other have only made them hate themselves and each other more. Neither fulfills the biblical role of husband or wife and neither likes the people they have become.

The examples of the destructive, unchristian behavior that can arise from a low self-image are endless. I have counseled women who neglect their children and become the total executive, not because they really want to but because they feel inadequate and are trying to prove that they can do it. They don't appear to have a low self-image, but they do, and that lack of a sense of self-worth drives them to abandon what they really want to do, namely, raise their children.

Then again, many women stay at home for the same reason. These women have talents they want to use in the marketplace, but they don't think they are intelligent enough or clever enough. Self-doubt can cause some people to act when they shouldn't, just to prove themselves; for others, self-doubt tends to cripple any constructive action.

* * *

Self-love or self-acceptance is not the same as self-worship. Self-worship actually issues forth into the opposite of a good self-image. Self-worship leads to arrogance and self-centeredness, whereas a good self-image enables self-forgetfulness and frees a person to focus on a task or on concern for another human being.

In the words of Kierkegaard:

> If anyone, therefore, will not learn from Christianity to love *himself* in the right way, then neither can he love his neighbor....To love one's self in the right way and to love one's neighbors are absolutely analogous concepts, are at the bottom one and the same...Hence the law is: "You shall love yourself as you love your neighbor when you love him as yourself."[3]

The kind of pride that is to be abhorred by the Christian is a false mock-up of a real self-worth. Pride denigrates the worth of others. Pride does not love. Pride enjoys seeing others fall and will promote itself over the fall of others. Pride always needs to outdo the other person because, underneath, pride is not really very sure of itself at all.

I don't see a lot of pride in my counseling office, but I do see people who are strong enough to seek change and humble enough to ask for it. At times I also see people who are sent by proud people, people who feel too insecure to come themselves because it might mean that something is wrong with them.

Humility is never a state of meek, self-denigrating nothingness. Real martyrs don't enjoy dying; they hate it. Because they are confident people, however, they *dare* to die for what they believe. Real humility takes courage. On an everyday level, humility simply means an absence from self-occupation so that we can attend to our appointed tasks. Humility requires freedom from self, and freedom from self indicates self-confidence. Real humility is, in every sense of the term, a dream block.

* * *

C. S. Lewis comments:

> Starting with the doctrine that every individuality is "of infinite value" we then picture God as a kind of employment committee whose business it is to find suitable careers for souls, square holes for square pegs. In fact, however, the value of the individual does not lie in him. He is capable of receiving value. He receives it by union with Christ.[4]

Once received, however, "If God is satisfied with the work the work may be satisfied with itself."[5]

I have noticed that when I do public speaking, which at times is God's "career" for me, if I am rested physically and confident about what I want to say, I forget myself when I speak. My focus is on the subject matter and on the connection I make between the topic and the audience. I don't worry about how I look, how I sound, or whether I'm succeeding. The task is my focus. Such times of speaking are always successful. Right here you combine the dimension of the physical, the psychological, and the spiritual. The result in this example is wholeness.

I get into trouble when I am self-conscious. When I focus on myself and how I am coming through, I never do as well. Ironically, self-confidence is a tool that can enable a freedom from thinking about self. Likewise, trusting in God can promote self-confidence, and self-confidence also makes it easier to trust God. The two are mutually supportive, not antithetical.

Furthermore, there is a difference between seeking God's approval and seeking others' approval. There is nothing wrong with liking people's approval of us. In public speaking, for example, when I can see that people are really hearing what I am saying, it is a very rewarding experience and not at all wrong. However, people do not always respond as we wish. Therefore, it is important to look for approval ultimately from God, for only He remains constant.

In talking about heavenly glory and the idea of wanting commendation, Lewis comments about the shock he experienced when he discovered that prominent Christians of the past, like Milton and Thomas Aquinas, interpreted heavenly glory to mean fame, or a good report:

> When I thought it over, I saw that this view was Scriptural; nothing can eliminate from the parable the divine accolade, "Well done, thou good and faithful servant." With that a good deal of what I had been thinking all my life fell down like a house of cards. I suddenly remembered that no one can enter heaven except as a child; and nothing is so obvious in a child – not in a conceited child but in a good child – as its great and undisguised pleasure in being praised. Not only in a child, either, but even in a dog or a horse. Apparently what I had mistaken for humility had, all these years, prevented me from understanding what is in fact the humblest, the most childlike, the most creaturely of pleasures – nay, the specific pleasure of the inferior: the pleasure of a beast before men, a child before its father, a pupil before his teacher, a creature before its Creator. ... [6]

As I was discussing some of these ideas over dinner with a friend, he said in surprise, "But should a Christian seek after success?"

Taken a little aback, because my friend is highly successful in sales, I replied, "How can you ask that? You're very successful yourself."

"I know," he replied, "but I always thought there was something kind of wrong with success. I just do it to survive."

"I just do it to survive." Yet he is doing something which he likes and in which he obviously excels. More than that, he is a very fair person who always puts his customer's needs over the sale. That's why people trust him, and that's why he should feel good about this task that God has entrusted to him. Some of our confusions over self-worth and self-hate do not make sense when we really look at them, and they are not very Christian.

Once again, psychologist Rollo May sums up this confusion very well when he says:

> In the circles where self-contempt is preached, it is of course never explained why a person should be so ill-mannered and inconsiderate as to force his company on other people if he finds it so dreary and deadening himself. And furthermore the multitude of contradictions are never adequately explained in a doctrine which advises that we should hate the one self, "I," and love all others, with the obvious expectation that they will love us, hateful creatures that we are; or that the more we hate ourselves, the more we love God who made the mistake, in an off moment, of creating this contemptible creature, "I."[7]

More succinctly, when commenting on a politician who dressed in tattered clothes in order to get the votes of the working man,

Socrates exclaimed, "Your vanity shows forth from every hole in your coat."[8]

* * *

Some of the worst atrocities in human history have been committed by people who were filled with self-doubt. Adolf Hitler killed six million Jews and five million others in the concentration camps alone. Yet as a child he was sickly, made poor grades in school, and by the time he was fifteen could remember seven changes of address and five different schools. His life passion was to become an artist, a dream that was shattered when he failed to pass the entrance test for the Vienna Academy of Fine Arts. After that, hunger, flophouses, and even jail were his companions until he found the place where he could be somebody – politics. The rest of the story is common knowledge, but the beginnings are steeped in self-hate and failure.

Certainly all of the atrocities of World War II, or even Germany's part in that war, cannot be attributed to Hitler's low self-image or to anyone else's. Economic factors, the course of history, and the presence of evil itself played major parts. Nevertheless, the self-hate of this insecure Austrian provided a major tool for the functioning of that evil. His own description of his growing hatred of the Jews is evidence of this: "Gradually I began to hate them," he commented. "For me this was the time of the greatest spiritual upheaval I have ever had to go though. I had ceased to be a *weak-kneed* cosmopolitan and become an anti-semite."[9]

In his own mind the weak Austrian had now become strong. Like many others, he mistook pride and, in his case, even racism for strength instead of the weakness that it truly was. If he had become truly confident, the world would have been spared much evil, for then he would not have felt the need to prove himself in such a pathological way.

* * *

It is important to realize that a good self-image does not guarantee morality. It does, however, enable the *growth* of morality. A good self-image helps a person have the courage to stand up for what he or she believes. At times it even helps a person trust in the enablement of God. If people are too filled with self-doubt, that doubt may keep them from believing in themselves or in God.

For many the counseling office can become a temporary safety zone of growth where they can develop a better sense of self-worth. Psychiatrist Viktor E. Frankl is fond of a Goethe quote: "If we take man as he is, we make him worse; if we take him as he ought to be, we help him become it."[10]

Paul Tournier comments: "If one thoughtlessly calls a child a liar, one makes him a liar, in spite of all of his aspirations towards honesty. ... Call a child stupid, and you make him stupid, incapable of showing what he has it in him to do."[11] What is true of the child is to some extent true of all of us who are adults.

To take people as they ought to be and can become should be the creed of all counseling and psychotherapy. In that atmosphere of acceptance and confrontation, the counseling office becomes a place that fosters growth and wholeness. It is a place where people assemble the building blocks of self-esteem, the various dimensions of what it means to become whole.

Whether or not a person develops a good self-image can determine the whole course of a life. In describing a desperate period of his life, the late Sammy Davis, Jr., told an interviewer in 1989, "I didn't like me. So it made all the sense in the world to me at the time that if you don't like yourself you destroy yourself."[12] After such insight and pain, to me it was a tribute to man's God-given potential for growth when Jesse Jackson could say at Mr. Davis's funeral, "He recycled pain into joy."

Counseling is in the business of recycling lives. In the safety zone of the counseling office, many people truly recycle pain into joy, failure into success, futility into meaning, and sorrow into understanding. The end result is dream blocks that can then be used for building dreams. The raw material of these dream blocks is a good self-image.

We are such stuff as dreams are made on ...

– William Shakespeare

Six

Dream Builders

Somehow Saturday always feels a little less like a workday to me than the other days I spend in my counseling office. It seems harder to get up in the morning and, like most people on Saturday, I tend to dress more casually. The routine of being a student and then a teacher dies hard. Actually for me it has never died! Yet my Saturdays are always busy because that is the best time for anyone who works nine to five to make a weekly counseling appointment. It's also great for kids.

This particular Saturday was filled with appointments, and I had only a short time off for lunch. Right before I took my noon break, I went into my waiting room and saw a short, rather heavyset man sitting there.

"May I help you?" I inquired.

"You don't know who I am, do you?" the man asked. Then he explained that he was the husband of Susan, a woman I was counseling. Immediately I remembered their situation.

Susan and her husband, Joe, had recently left a small church where they had been members for the last ten years. The church was legalistic and required that all of its members be under the total control of the pastor and the board of elders. Members were not allowed to have anything to do with anyone outside the church, even relatives; they were obligated to live on a tight budget and hand over all other money to the church; and their children were educated in a church-controlled private school. Finally, after getting married and having four children, Susan and Joe had left the church.

When Susan first consulted me a few weeks earlier, she was undergoing a kind of culture shock. She had no friends; she had a job outside her home for the first time and was afraid of losing it because she was so nervous; and she and Joe were arguing a lot over the rightness of what they had done. Joe wouldn't come in to see me because I was a woman and also because he was afraid that a professional counselor might corrupt his spiritual beliefs.

On this particular Saturday Joe had reached a point of desperation. He had left home early that morning. First he had driven to the beach in hopes of finding a sense of perspective. Next he had called a friend from his former church. The man hung up on him. Then he called his brother who lived across the country. All his brother would say was that he thought Joe had been crazy to go to such a church in the first place. He certainly didn't understand any guilt over leaving. Thus, in a state of total desperation that obliterated any fears he had of being corrupted by me, Joe arrived in my waiting room. "Can you talk to me?" he asked.

The best I could do was give him my lunchtime, which amounted to a tight forty minutes if I let the rest of the day run about ten minutes late. I knew that I had to see him or he might never seek help from anyone again. I realized that in his state of desperation I could not turn him away or make a future appointment. Yet as he started to explain his feelings of guilt and isolation, I felt that we needed a number of sessions, not less than one, to sort out his feelings and start to put the pieces together. It was crisis counseling. I had to make something work *now*.

Within ten minutes I realized that most of the problems he was presenting related to the Bible and theology. For now the spiritual dimension was paramount. Did the Bible teach that there was to be a small, select group of Christians who should isolate themselves from other Christians? Did the Bible support the kind of unlove that was shown by the former friend who had just hung up on him that morning? "How can I know that my decision to leave this church was a right one?" he asked.

For the time, I gave up on most psychological solutions and just reinforced his own conclusion that what he was doing had biblical endorsement. He still had God. Here was a man who had been so damaged by so-called Christians that his self-esteem had been shattered. In a very few minutes he received a great deal of help just from being affirmed.

For Joe on that Saturday noon, my counseling office took on all the characteristics of a safety zone. It was secure. It provided refuge from a world that was at that time in Joe's life very hostile. It offered a place of recovery from a very shattering experience. It was available for his needs.

Over the next few weeks the rebuilding came quickly. Even the psychological repair of the damage to his confidence required only a few sessions. Mainly, in his case, all he needed to know was what any Christian with a basic knowledge of the Bible could have pointed out to him. He and God were okay in their relationship.

Susan and Joe both needed a short period of support and some suggestions on the practical rebuilding of their lives and those of their family. They needed friends, a new church, schools, and a whole way of life that they had almost forgotten existed. Counseling also helped Joe and Susan to keep the Christian beliefs that were so vital to them while they shed the extreme teaching of the group with whom they had been associated for ten years. In years to come the help they received in those few weeks of counseling enabled them to assist others who left the same church group and who, like them, felt desolate and guilt-ridden.

After having their dream blocks crushed and broken for years, Joe and Susan once again became dream builders. Once her confidence reached a certain level, Susan went back to teaching, a profession she had dropped at the church's orders. Joe redeveloped a hobby of cabinetmaking and eventually helped delinquent boys by teaching them this skill. Both of them had raised their self-images through counseling. Then, as they developed their lives and succeeded, that self-esteem increased even more.

* * *

Each of us has dreams. Sometimes those dreams are so hidden within us that we are barely aware of them. Along the way people may have made us believe that only the young have dreams or, worse still, that it is wrong to dream at all. But even if we are aware of our dreams, if we have too much self-doubt, or if we have not developed some skills that enable us to handle relationships with friends in the present and memories of the past, we will find ourselves forgetting our dreams and lowering our expectations of life to simple survival.

Self-esteem is a basic material in dream blocks, but self-esteem can be elusive. It is vital to good mental health, and yet it can be fragile and fluctuating. Paradoxically, it can be sturdy, too. It never ceases to amaze me how fast a damaged self-image can be restored and how quickly it can be once again dashed to the ground. In the case of Joe and Susan, for example, once they left their church, they felt, understandably, guilty and relieved at the same time. Then they met with blatant rejection from all their friends, which in turn made them feel more guilty. Their children were upset, which increased their sense of guilt.

For a while they didn't know whether to feel guilty for having been part of such a church or guilty because they had left. This frustration further lowered their self-images. The vicious circle went on. Every change, rejection, failure, and sharp word of criticism just intensified the downward spiral of their self-esteem. Even God seemed to be rejecting them!

For Joe and Sue, counseling provided a safety zone of support and growth that reversed the process. Because we were all of the Christian faith, I was able to reinforce them spiritually as well as psychologically. Had they been Jewish, for example, and had their problems been related to their Jewish faith, I might have needed the help of a rabbi. With Joe and Sue, spiritual support started the reversal of the downward spiral of their self-esteem, so that it now began to spiral up. After that beginning, each friend they added to their lives, each success, each insight they gained into their own God-given gifts and talents, each kind word, each tool for living, all these continued that spiral upward until Joe and Susan were ready to continue their growth without the safety zone of counseling. They had learned skills and been given tools that enabled them to rebuild the raw material of their lives, the dream blocks of self-esteem. Once again they became dream builders.

Most of the people I counsel do not present the same magnitude of spiritual problems that Joe and Susan had. Still, sometimes the lines between people's spiritual needs, emotional problems, physical ailments, and even something as simple as the need for friendship are very hard to distinguish. All the dimensions contained within the broader dimensions of body, mind, and spirit come together in brokenness as well as in wholeness.

* * *

In his insightful book *The Doctor and the Soul*, Viktor E. Frankl portrays the unique problems of those who seek the refuge of the counseling office for problems that are more specifically part of the spiritual dimension rather than the psychological:

> People are constantly coming to us with problems such as, what is the meaning of their lives.... Medicine, and psychiatry in particular, has thereby been compelled to cope with a new field.... Medical ministry [or, I might add, counseling ministry] does not aspire to be a

substitute for the proper cure of souls which is
practiced by the minister or priest.[1]

In essence, people today have tremendous problems with
meaning. These problems pervade their feelings about their personal
worth, their dealings with suffering, and their sense of values. Yet
in the middle of a spiritual desert, there is a tendency to seek out
the psychiatrist, the psychologist, or the counselor rather than the
priest, the minister, or the rabbi.

To me the reason lies primarily in the definition of the counseling
office as a safety zone. The other day a patient said to me, "When I
went to my pastor, he condemned me and told me I was sinning and
not being a good wife. Thank you for not doing that."

In actuality, the woman is a "good" wife and a "good" woman. She
and her husband even have a fairly stable relationship. However, her
self-esteem problems make her overly sensitive to his criticism, an
oversensitivity that was not improved by the condemnation and
harshness she received from her pastor. Quietly, she simply left the
church and sought professional help.

If her pastor had viewed his counseling office as a place to build
people up, as well as a place of confrontation if that was required,
and if that confrontation had been done in love, then she might
not ever have left his church. Furthermore, had he been willing,
professional counseling could have been done with the support of
the pastor's spiritual counsel. Dream blocks of self-esteem would
have been built rather than destroyed.

Paul Tournier, who was a solid Christian as well as a psychiatrist,
makes what is to me a sad comment on the subject of the relationship
of many who seek professional counseling and the church to which
they belong. In speaking of the counseling office as a place, Dr.
Tournier says:

Through us and our place, the patient is attached
once more to society, and often also to God

and the Church, which then become for him the best possible place. Nevertheless I ought to say that it is often very difficult for a patient who has been cured, or at least undergone an improvement in his condition, to feel at home in the Church, even if he wants to. He finds it so impersonal, so cold and conventional, after the stirring experiences he has had in the psychotherapist's consulting room.[2]

This should not be, for divine love, lived out through God's people should surpass the human love found in any counseling office. This viewpoint also raises serious questions about the safety of the director-directee approach to counseling within the church and the ever present problems in dual relationships.

* * *

In the parable of the prodigal son, his sin, and his subsequent return to his father's house, there is repentance of sin, but there is no further reproach, no period of probation, no "I told you so." Yet no one, including the prodigal son himself, denied that the basis of his problems had been sin. He had caused his own problems.

Most people who seek psychological counseling, however, have not caused their own problems by blatant wrongdoing. They just hurt. Certainly their welcome from the church should be as warm as that given to the prodigal son. Above all other places, the church and the pastor's consulting room should be places of affirmation and safety. Affirmation is one function of the safety zone of counseling. Affirmation builds people; affirmation reverses the downward cycle of low self-esteem.

Recently, someone said to me in a careless afterthought, "You know, if I wanted to be sure that others understood my pain, I'd probably pick a bar to go to rather than a church. At least, I wouldn't be criticized."

There is nothing so comforting on this earth as the love of God poured out to us from Christians who are filled with God's love. But when that love is absent, Christian standards can begin to feel harsh indeed. If some seek comfort in bars instead of in Christian fellowship, then we who are Christians need to examine the quality of our love.

This in no way implies that we must lower our standards of what is right and wrong. But it does mean that we allow God to love other people through us, whether or not they agree with us. To love the unlovely, to love the unresponsive: this is the truest test of the reality of our love.

Consistent with this way of thinking, just because we disagree with someone, or even when we feel they are morally wrong, does not excuse unlove or poor manners. In the words of Amy Carmichael, "…if anyone is inclined to think that rudeness and honesty run together, and politeness and insincerity, I will tell you what I have found: The strongest, bravest, truest people I ever knew were (are) the most gentle-mannered. Good manners are not among the things that do not matter. Can we imagine our Lord Jesus ever being rude?"[3]

God is our ultimate Affirmer. He made us in His image and redeemed us with His blood. His affirmation alone imputes great value to the worth of each individual human being. In the words of Helmut Thielicke, "For God does not love us because we are so valuable; rather we are valuable because God loves us."[4]

God's view of man, furthermore, places a strong obligation upon the members of His church to become affirmers. Read any of the greetings from Paul to members of the early church, for example, and you will find commendation and praise of a whole host of people. Surrounded by active persecution, these people needed each other's affirmation if they were to continue building the church in the middle of such great trouble. Providing a theological basis for such affirmation, Thielicke continues, "Because the other person is valuable to God he compels me to show reverence. Therefore my love is no longer addressed to an unstable function, to what in any given moment I can or cannot find to be 'valuable for me' in the other person."[5]

In describing the affirming atmosphere of a large hospital in Germany, Paul Tournier adds to our understanding of the practical potential of affirmation from even just one individual when he quotes its head physician as saying:

> I think I can say that my hospital is pervaded by a personal spirit, but I believe we owe this almost entirely to a single person – our Sister Superior, who is so profoundly human that everyone whose life she touches feels that he is considered a person, feels himself becoming a person.[6]

That each human being is valuable is basic to any counseling that sets out to help rebuild lives. When affirmation from friends is not enough to restore a damaged self-image, or when that affirmation is not forthcoming, then it becomes the province of the professional counselor.

* * *

Affirmation must be based on truth, however, or it builds upon a very shaky foundation indeed. Furthermore, affirmation is usually a simple process that may involve sorting out facts, evaluating situations, and simply telling someone that he or she is okay.

Not long ago a man in his early thirties told me in poignant detail how he used to come home from school and ask his mother, "What is wrong with me? Why do the other kids tease me?"

Today John is handsome, a successful architect, and happily married. Yet underneath all that success he harbored a nagging feeling that he was not worthwhile. He sought counseling and asked me the same question he had asked his mother years earlier, "What is wrong with me?"

Together we figured out that because John had been a small, shy boy who was bad at sports but exceptionally good academically, he stood out and became the perfect victim. Then, because no one ever taught him how to deal with teasing, he responded in all the wrong ways. He lost his temper, cried, and hid from his tormentors. These reactions just fueled more teasing. After all, a bully always enjoys a victim who reacts.

As John began to realize why he had been teased and saw that when he was a child there had been no relationship between his real worth and what he considered then to be his unpopularity, he was free to evaluate himself more honestly in the present. He learned to value strengths, like his creativity as an architect, the respect of his friends, his faithfulness to his children, and the love of a good wife. Ironically, he grew closer to God, too. That deep gut feeling that no one could really like him, including God, had almost disappeared. John was free enough from self-occupation to grow and to reach out to others. Paradoxically, because he liked himself more, he thought of himself less. He didn't have to worry about whether he was okay.

* * *

People who have low self-images may not be able to see the truth about themselves, even when all the facts are obvious. At such a point the pastor, the friend, or the professional counselor is needed to help these people see themselves more clearly. A woman who was a very competent teacher consulted me because of a number of relationships that all seemed to be going badly. On the surface there were at least two possibilities: either Brenda was offending people and didn't wear well in long-term friendships or she was choosing the wrong people as friends. Some of the differences between her and two of her friends revolved around money.

Brenda had borrowed two thousand dollars from a friend in order to buy a car for transportation to her first teaching job. The friend asked her to pay a hundred a month, then two hundred, then two hundred fifty. The escalating payments were seriously restricting Brenda in other areas. Other bills went unpaid. Messages from bill collectors began to appear on her answering machine. Thoughts of what she owed kept her awake at night. She could no longer afford dinner with friends, which made her feel isolated. Compounding her anxiety, the friend's demands to keep paying more persisted and worried her. Then, when she could least afford it, counseling became a necessity because of all the anxiety.

We began by talking about possible sources of additional income. Then I asked her how much longer the payments would continue. "My friend says that if I go to four hundred a month I'll be paid up in four more months," she replied.

When she said this, my mind blurred, and yet momentarily I went along with her thinking: four months would be tough, but she should focus beyond four months to the day when her debt would be paid and she would be free of that particular pressure. Then, suddenly, it all became clear to me. Brenda hadn't even kept track of her payments. She had just trusted her friend's word. In truth, she had already overpaid the debt she owed. In four months, at four hundred dollars a month, her friend would have owed Brenda more than two thousand dollars! Brenda reacted with relief first and then anger. "I just assumed that she was right and I was wrong," she said.

In an ironic sort of role reversal, she then explained that her other close friend, also a teacher, owed *her* five hundred dollars. The friend had recently called to ask how much Brenda wanted her to pay each month. The friend even suggested fifty dollars a month. Brenda's question to me was a hesitant "Do you think I could dare to ask her for fifty dollars a month?"

Brenda is a good example of a person who is honest and tries to be a good friend. Because she doesn't respect herself, she chooses people who take advantage of her. She doesn't see this, however, and assumes that the resultant problems have to be her fault. She doesn't trust herself enough to feel that she could be right. For her, counseling needs to help her evaluate her worth more honestly and see the value she has and, once that is accomplished, to encourage her to improve her choice of friends. As this occurs, the building blocks of self-esteem will be formed, and she will be free enough from herself to build her dreams.

* * *

Affirmation, whether it becomes part of the counseling process or remains in the province of friendship, is simply reinforcement of the fact that God doesn't make junk. The late Walter Trobisch made a great contribution in his writings on self-esteem. In *Love Yourself*, Trobisch drew from his missionary background to give a clear example in the area of self-esteem and affirmation:

> When I write this I have to think of my African friends. It seems so much easier for them to accept themselves than for us Westerners. I am reminded of one of my best friends, an African man who is rather short. A well-meaning person

once suggested to him that he wear shoes with higher heels in order to appear taller.

This was almost an offense to my friend. Hadn't God made him short? Why should he seek to change what God had created? He had accepted himself as he was and loved himself with his height. I am sure this complete self acceptance is one of the reasons that he can be such a good friend to me.[7]

Although a change in self-perception is one aspect of changing one's self-image, often a change in behavior is required also. Brenda, the teacher who owed her friend money, for example, needed to change her perception of her own worth as well as change her way of dealing with both her use of money and her choice of friends. She needed to realize that she was worth having healthy friends. One symptom of low self-esteem is that very capable, worthwhile people sometimes choose irresponsible friends. They feel that no one they respect would want to be their friend, or they feel that by choosing unstable friends they don't have to feel threatened and can even feel superior.

For those who feel that most of their friendships are unsatisfactory, it is important to ask, Do I choose people who always fail me because I feel unworthy of more reliable friends? Are these the only people who will be my friends because I don't give much back in a friendship? If the answer to the former is "Yes," you may need a whole set of new friends, and the problems in your friendships may relate more to the kinds of people you associate with rather than your failure as a friend. If the answer to the latter question is "Yes," you need to learn to be a better friend yourself. In either case, whether you choose poorly or behave poorly, self-esteem is probably a major factor. One thing I am sure of is that most people choose friends who basically share the same level of mental health.

For this reason it is wise to make sure that one's self-image is secure before making major life decisions, such as choosing a life partner. As I said to one patient, "Six months ago you would have chosen a fairly damaged individual. Today you would make a better choice. Six months from now, you will probably choose a partner with whom you truly want to spend the rest of your life."

* * *

Sometimes changing a person's self-image means going beyond just choosing better friends or dealing more efficiently with life. It can mean facing wrongdoing. According to Martin Luther, to *repent* is to do so no more. That is the best definition I've ever heard, and it works. The businessman whom I saw who was sleeping with his wife's best friend and was fraudulent in his business practices also didn't like himself. At first he thought that counseling was supposed to make him realize that he was really a fine man, regardless of his behavior. "You're supposed to make me like myself," he said to me. The problem was that he wasn't a fine man!

Certainly he had some good qualities of personality and a keen business sense. He knew that without any help from me. Because of the moral fiber of his life-style, however, his self-esteem could never be strong without massive changes in his behavior. From just a practical point of view, if he continued in his present direction, he could look forward to the destruction of his marriage, his family, and his business and perhaps to a change of address to jail!

To have simply developed an honest perception of himself would have lowered his self-image more than it would have raised it. Forgiveness and change had to be the basis for a better self-image. Any psychological mind trip that attempts to make a person feel good about doing bad is not sound, either psychologically or spiritually, and it doesn't work on any long-term basis.

* * *

Sometimes, however, the need to change is not based upon dealing with wrongdoing as much as it involves certain changes in behavior that just work better. Although procrastination, lack of organization, untidiness, shyness, and many other similar characteristics may have nothing to do with sin, they often demand change if a person's self-image is to improve. These qualities are not wrong in themselves, but they often make people feel bad about themselves. Shyness can isolate us, untidiness can keep us from hospitality or make us feel inadequate when we do entertain, and procrastination can make us lose jobs or alienate us from friends.

Christianity provides the solution to issues involving sin, but Christians are often the least understanding in areas that relate to imperfection. In our confusion, we tend to merge the two and thus develop the "confess your depression" brand of counseling that ends up being destructive to so many.

C. S. Lewis gives the best example I have seen of the difference between those things in our personality that are simply imperfect and yet still affect our self-image and those ways of behavior that lower our self-image because they are sinful.

In his book *Mere Christianity* Lewis gives an apt illustration of the difference between situations that involve human frailty and those that require moral choice. Three men go to war. One has a certain fear of the danger involved, but he rises above that fear and shows courage. The other two have such great fears regarding war that they cannot fight. Their fears go beyond the rational to the irrational. Moral choice alone cannot conquer the fears. At that point a psychoanalyst treats the two and cures them. The psychological problem ends and the moral problem starts. Now that they are cured, they can respond with relief but still refuse to make the choice to fight. On the other hand, now that they are cured, they can make the choice to go ahead and do what is right.

Says Lewis, "The bad psychological material is not a sin but a disease. It does not have to be repented of, but to be cured.... Human beings judge one another by their external actions. God judges them by their moral choices."[8]

To summarize, again in the words of Lewis, "Fear is horrid but there's no reason to be ashamed of it. Our Lord was afraid of Gethsemane."[9] But our Lord never sinned.

I once saw an eleven-year-old boy who seemed to be having problems in every area of his life. His family couldn't get along with him, he fought with his classmates, and his grades had fallen dramatically from the previous year. After a few sessions that clearly pointed out his lack of self-confidence but didn't give a clue as to its source, I asked what proved to be the vital question, "Why do you always wear a baseball cap?"

In typical preteen fashion he mumbled, "I don't know."

"Would you care to take it off for just a moment?" I asked.

After considerable persuasion, Justin took off his cap, and I knew why he wore the cap. Without the cap Justin's hair stood straight up! He quickly replaced the hat and told me that for the past year he had refused to take it off for just that reason. His hair stood up, and everyone teased him. Teasing for *wearing* the cap was less painful. For one year Justin's grades and social relationships had plummeted because of his hair. Justin wanted to be a doctor. With his current academic progress that goal was becoming unattainable. He had stopped building toward his dreams.

Justin's mother either cut Justin's hair herself or sent him to the cheapest barber she could find. I suggested someone more qualified, in lieu of paying even more to me for additional counseling. She agreed. The next and last time I saw Justin he was happy and relaxed. All his self-esteem needed was a good haircut!

* * *

It was important, too, for Justin himself to be willing to take off his cap and tell about being teased – and not to be forced to do either. Even the smallest child should feel a sense of privacy about his or her inner thoughts. Only where major issues are involved, like drugs or physical danger, should the adult world forcibly intrude. In this way the child retains the right to be a person. The child grows up with a sense of self-respect.

As a small child of about five, I remember feeling intimidated one afternoon when my mother asked me questions about my relationship with God. I didn't disagree with her beliefs. Very early in life I had turned my life over to Jesus Christ. I was definitely a Christian. Nevertheless, I remember so clearly standing in the dining room and thinking, *They can make me do whatever they want. But they can't look into my mind. My thoughts are my own.* It was undoubtedly my way of asserting myself as a person, separate from my parents, even if I did agree with them. It was my way of having a private world in the sometimes not so private world of a child.

In order to develop and maintain a good self-image, every human being, regardless of age, has to maintain feelings of dignity. To help people do that is to be an affirmer. For example, just because someone who is aged may be physically helpless does not mean that his or her private life should be openly discussed without regard for their feelings. Children too old to be undressed in front of other people, and too young to protest, should have their needs attended to in private. Criticism of employees, the clarification of a problem with a friend, and confrontation in general should never be done in the presence of people who are not involved in the problem.

The counseling office, above all other places, should always be a place of dignity and safety. Especially in this place of rebuilding and growth, each individual should feel the right to reveal himself at his own pace. No one should feel intimidated to tell more than he can or foolish if he cannot at first feel complete trust. Trust is earned, especially the trust that must eventually exist between the counselor and the counselee in this very intimate human relationship.

I remember a teenage girl who was sent to me by a social worker so that I could determine her needs in terms of foster care and adoption. She had been brutally molested for a number of years. When she walked into my office, she said, "I've already told the police what happened. I don't want to talk about it again." I agreed, and we talked about where she wanted to live and what she wanted to do with her life.

Halfway through the hour she asked, "Do you mind if I tell you what happened? I'd like you to know." When she told me what were probably the most intimate details of her life so far, it was her decision to share them with me; it was her act of trust. She had been allowed the dignity of choice. The safety zone of counseling had not been just a place where she found solutions to her problems; it had been a place where her self-image was reinforced by providing an atmosphere of respect for her as an individual.

* * *

Not every self-image problem is deep-seated or deals with wrongdoing. In the marriage counseling I do, I have often thought many marital problems would never develop if the husband would occasionally take care of the baby in the evening while his wife went shopping, or if the wife would encourage her husband to take time out to do something relaxing for a few minutes after he gets home from work. A cold drink served to someone who is working outside in the heat, a thank-you for a task well done, a few minutes of time spent listening, even when you don't feel like it – such trivia make up the fabric of domestic life; and both giving and receiving such seemingly small acts of consideration elevate a person's sense of self-worth.

If rebuilding a damaged self-image in the privacy of a counseling office teaches us anything about technique, it teaches us that self-confidence is most effectively learned through receiving the understanding of another human being and giving love to others around us. Then the more I like this person called *me*, the more I am free from focusing on me. A person who has a strong self-image doesn't have to always prove that he or she is right. A person with a strong self-image doesn't have to be afraid to say, "I'm sorry."

An effective counselor sees the patient for all of his or her potential. An attractive young woman walked into my office last week and gave a highly intelligent explanation of why she was seeking counseling. What I saw and heard was intelligent, attractive, and well-mannered. Yet she summarized her needs by describing herself as stupid and ugly. When her perception of herself more closely resembles that of those who know her, she will no longer need counseling. She will have acquired sound building material with which to develop her life.

G. K. Chesterton once wrote of Saint Francis:

> He deliberately did not see the mob for the men.... He only saw the image of God multiplied but never monotonous. To him a man was always a man and did not disappear in a dense crowd any more than in a desert. He honoured all men; that is he not only loved but respected them all ... there was never a man who looked into those brown burning eyes without being certain that Francis Bernardone was really interested in him; in his own inner individual

> life from the cradle to the grave; that he himself
> was being valued and taken seriously....[10]

In my bedroom I have large floor-to-ceiling windows. Through these windows I can look out and see the mountains in the distance and the trees that line my street. Across the street are two particularly beautiful trees that, unlike so many trees in California, change with the seasons. A few years ago the man who lived across the street decided to put a low wall across the front of his yard. He brought in a supply of bricks and mixed some mortar. Bricks were spread all around. Then he began, brick by brick, to build the wall.

At first, all it amounted to was one row of bricks cemented together, and then another row just like it. The whole process took several days, brick by brick. After a while, a pattern began to emerge. This was not going to be an ordinary brick wall, after all. The bricks began to be staggered rather than just set evenly on top of each other until, at the end, a very artistic brick wall surrounded the walkway and the two beautiful trees.

Dream builders do something very similar with their lives. First they have a dream. Then they build that dream into reality with dream blocks – attitudes, talents, skills, resources which make their specific dreams come true. Sometimes the dream blocks become damaged and need to be repaired. Often they need to be reinforced. Whatever the cost, for the dream builders, the building goes on. Then, someday before they know it, the form of something far more wonderful than they imagined may emerge. The dream will have become concrete.

I have learned silence from the talkative, toleration from the intolerant, and kindness from the unkind; yet strange, I am ungrateful to those teachers.

– Kahil Gibran

SEVEN

DREAM BASHERS

On our last family outing before my father's death, my mother, father, and I went to the ocean late one afternoon. Equipped with beach towels and several cans of chilled soft drinks, we found a place on the sand close to the ocean. For a while my mother and I walked along the beach, picking up shells, and wading in the shallow water. Until we joined him, my father sat on the shore, alone on a beach towel, just looking out at the sea.

After his death, I remembered the scene vividly. My father had rolled up his denim pants to his knees and taken off his blue cotton shirt. As he sat, drinking in the last rays of the setting sun, the wind was blowing through his white hair. Yet his sun-tanned shoulders and face, along with his strong physique, belied his seventy-four years. The sea was his love, a feeling my mother shared and that they both passed on to me early in my life. It was appropriate that this beach would be our last real place on earth together.

It was sunset and the sun was low on the horizon. Its bright orange rays dipped through the distant line between ocean and sky, while within a few feet of where we were sitting the waves came in gently toward us and then retreated, leaving behind a glassy sheet of sand covered by an abundance of white foam.

My mother and I joined my father, and the three of us sat silently watching the tide, coming in and out with an almost hypnotic rhythm, and the foam, which by now had spread out like soapsuds across most of the beach. Distracted for a moment from the scene, I turned to my father to show him a shell with an interesting formation. Then within seconds the tranquil scene was shattered by a series of stronger waves that covered us and our things with seawater and sand. We scrambled to our feet, retrieved purses and shoes, and concentrated on escaping further drenching. We moved farther up the beach. Ordinary life had returned.

* * *

Life has its built-in disappointments, some of them as small as the fluctuating tide of the sea and some as monumental as a terminal illness. Whether the disturbance comes from nature or from another human being, sometimes life, like the ocean tide, interrupts our lives in an unavoidable way. Not long ago I walked into my office waiting room in time to hear howls of rage from a small boy who had just built a very high tower out of blocks, only to have it kicked into oblivion by his older sister. The young dream builder had just had his dream cut down by a dream basher in a way reminiscent of Lucy in Charles Schulz's cartoons when she says, "Can't you ever do anything right, Charlie Brown?"

On the level of the trivial, the disturbance may be relatively minor. Some days are just too hot, or too cold. For most of us, just when we think we are caught up on bills or have our home in shape, an unexpected expense arises or the paint begins to peel. Our youngest son, who we hoped would be a star basketball player like his father, turns out to be interested in water-skiing. Real estate soars just when we go to buy a house; or when we find that perfect mother-of-the-bride outfit, we discover that the store is out of our size.

Certain big issues, too, like the inevitability of death or the certainty of earthquakes in California, are unavoidable. Although we can try to drive carefully to avoid a car accident, and take all possible precautions, sometimes a drunken driver may cross over the center line and leave us no chance at all to avoid a collision.

The examples of unavoidable unpleasantness or even disaster are many. What I learn in my counseling office, however, is that many people do not distinguish between the unavoidable problems of life and those situations that are very avoidable for them as individuals. In addition to the problems of a low self-image, the most common characteristic of people who seek professional counseling seems to be the feeling that they have somehow lost control of their lives. People may feel so overextended, so dominated by others' opinions, or so enslaved by their own negative emotions that they truly feel that control of their lives is no longer theirs.

*　*　*

Building upon a foundation of good self-esteem, becoming whole is facilitated by the act of declaring. To declare is to state one's boundaries. It does *not* mean arguing, debating, convincing, attacking, or pleading for permission. One declares for oneself, not for someone else. "I am going to bed at ten" does not mean that someone else must go to bed at the same time. "I go to church every Sunday" does not mean telling everyone else that they must do the same or even asking permission to do so.

Declaring sounds almost simplistic, yet it is an important psychological dimension of wholeness which can be addressed in therapy sessions. For those who have spent their lives hoping that if they could just change the world around them their own world could calm down, the technique is difficult to acquire but lifesaving in its potential. A woman I had not seen in several years called me and said, "Life around me has been worse since I last saw you. But I'm better now than I've ever been. What made the difference was when you said: 'You can't wait for the world around you to change, even if they are the ones who need to. You must change.' I've done that," she said, "and that has made all the difference."

Declaring preserves the ability to do what we have been placed on this earth to do. It results in clearing away the unwarranted demands of others that keep us from our task. It often involves saying "No" to what is good in order to do what is better. Declaring is not selfish; it is self-preserving. Declaring means stating God-given boundaries.

Every human being is placed on this earth for a specific purpose. If we are to fulfill that purpose, we cannot afford to go off on every tangent that comes along, just because we can't say "No." Indeed, we could reason that we have an obligation to focus on our God-given course and not allow ourselves to be distracted from that course, even by an activity that is in itself worthwhile.

Psychiatrist G. L. Harrington, previously referred to in this book, once related an incident that occurred when he was a resident in training. He was assigned to a number of patients in a hospital psychiatric ward. One man had been totally unreachable, and previous residents had given up on him. This history only spurred on my friend. He decided that he would reach this man above all others.

Day after day he increased his therapy time with his patient. Soon he spent his lunchtime with the man and then dinner. Then he came back after hours. Even though he had a wife and children at home, he ended up spending eight to nine hours daily, apart from his normal hours, with this man. He reached the point where he felt as if the man and he were imprisoned in a box, and he was trying now to cure the man so that he himself could also get out of the box. His comment to me was, "I became as crazy as he was."

He had lost control over his life, not out of selfishness or greed, but because he had tried too hard to help this other human being. The solution for my friend was not to try to cure the man so that he himself could get free but, rather, to jump out of the box himself and then declare the boundaries within which he as a healthy person could help this other person toward mental health.

* * *

There are basically two kinds of people in this world: dream builders and dream bashers. Sometimes we are a little of each, but most of us tend to be more one than the other. Dream bashing is the enemy of dream building. The weapon against dream bashing is declaring.

From early in life all of us have known dream bashers; for dream bashing starts in childhood, usually in ways that seem small to an adult but are heartbreaking to a child. I have always been fond of animals and have rarely been without a cat and a dog. My first dog, Jack, a huge Saint Bernard-collie combination, was my constant companion and playmate from the time I was about four years old. One day when Jack and I were playing in the backyard, he spontaneously licked my arm. The incident was of no importance. Jack often licked me. On this occasion, however, my playmate, who was several years older than I and perhaps was practicing that wisdom on me, said, "He's not doing that because he loves you; he just likes the salt on your skin."

That is the first vivid incident of dream bashing that I remember, and its irritating memory has followed me through life. On some half-conscious level, many times when my current dog jumps up and kisses me, I think, "Remember, this isn't love; he just likes the salt on your skin." Dream bashers make their imprint!

* * *

Last week I was watching a video portrayal of Mark Twain's *Life on the Mississippi.* As I watched it, I realized how much my present enjoyment was enhanced by a former college professor of mine. Leon Howard was a Guggenheim scholar and a well-known authority in several areas of American literature, but to me he was much more than that. To me he was a dream builder, for he taught me to understand and love literature in the same way that another scholar-professor, James Emerson Phillips, taught me to understand and love Shakespeare.

I don't even remember the names of most of my college professors, but every now and then I had a dream builder, and I remember those names. James Bouey shared his fascination with the biology of living creatures. Ellis Levine didn't just teach me German; he taught me confidence as well. There were others, like the professor who made me write a thousand-word essay on Humpty-Dumpty and perhaps in so doing gave me my first surge of confidence toward writing.

Not too many college professors stand out in my memory as dream builders. Most were in the middle, not terribly inspiring and yet not dream bashers either. Then there were a few real dream bashers. It was the dream builders, however, who left a positive imprint on the lives of their students that far exceeded the scope of the immediate classroom. Long after we left those classrooms, many of us continued to learn and grow in the directions in which these professors had started us.

* * *

Actually kicking over someone's sand castle isn't necessary to be a dream basher. Dream bashing can be subtle. To a student who brings home his first set of good grades, a dream-bashing statement says, "That's wonderful. I'm proud of you. But it's too bad you had to wait until tenth grade to do it." For the young bride who's learning to cook, a dream-bashing compliment would be "This is great! It's the first dinner I've really enjoyed." Everyone who's ever dieted can relate to the dream-bashing quality of, "That's a beautiful new dress. It doesn't make you look so heavy."

In addition to fending off the dream bashers in our lives, it is important for each of us not to become our own personal dream basher by denigrating our own worth. "I can't do anything right," for example, is a personal dream-bashing attitude. Some people are actually better dream builders for other people than they are for themselves. They point out positive things in the lives of others, while at the same time they feel that they themselves have no worth at all.

* * *

Most of us intuitively recognize the difference between a dream basher and a dream builder. If our self-esteem is at all sturdy, we avoid the former and gravitate toward the latter. A young man had failed to be accepted into a specialized training program because he failed the English test that was given prior to acceptance. One high school English teacher stood out in his mind as someone he could approach for advice.

"I never studied in high school," he explained to her when he went back and visited. The school day was over, and the two were chatting together in the empty classroom. The teacher asked Ben what the test had involved. It turned out to be based on a few simple concepts of grammar.

"I don't think I can ever catch up enough to pass the test," Ben continued, doing a simple version of dream bashing on himself.

The teacher, who had been a dream builder in the lives of many of her students, challenged Ben. "Give me one hour of your undivided attention, and I am sure you will go back and pass the test with flying colors." If the teacher had been a dream basher instead of a dream builder, she might have chided Ben for not studying in the past. Instead, she saw the potential for the future. She fulfilled the old maxim: "He has the right to criticize who has the heart to help."

Ben spent the next hour learning what he had never really learned before. Now he, too, had a dream, and learning English grammar had become part of fulfilling that dream. A few weeks later Ben passed his exam and entered his training program.

* * *

A person who lives an undeclared life is likely to be angry, frustrated, and ultimately burned-out. To be undeclared is to feel that you can never say "No." To be undeclared means yielding your own priorities to those that other people set for you. Rather than basing decisions on what is right for your life at any given time, to live undeclared is to let go of the control of your life – not to God where it belongs, but to people to whom you cannot say "No." It becomes a matter of "I can't say no," rather than "I believe this is the right course for my life."

The best example I have ever heard that defines *declaring* came through word of mouth to me and relates to the wife of the late General Douglas MacArthur. According to the story, people had been after her throughout her adult life to share stories, facts, and anecdotes about the general. Her answer remained the same: "When I married the general, he was already a four-star general. I determined then that I would not grant interviews, make speeches, or write books. That has held me in good stead for all these years, and I intend to stand by that decision." The statement doesn't explain; it doesn't ask permission. It closes the door, ever so politely but firmly. It allows no room for debate. A person would have to be pretty pushy to try that door twice. It is a declaration.

* * *

Some people I see in counseling sessions avoid confronting frustrating situations in their lives by saying, "It's okay. I can handle it if it doesn't get too bad." Usually they mean that it's harder to declare to that adult son, who lives in their home and wakes them up at two in the morning with his radio, than it is to endure the discomfort. Or, in another example, if they declare to the spouse who makes fun of them at parties or always complains about their way of dealing with money but will never sit down and talk about it, they feel then that somehow the situation will become even more intolerable. And so they continue on, silently, bitterly. They fight periodically, but they never declare.

One day, probably arising out of desperation combined with reading too many Agatha Christie mystery books, I turned to such a person and asked, "Knowing that small amounts of arsenic will not kill you but will just gradually make you sick, would you accept your weekly cup of tea or coffee in this office if you knew that it contained ever so small an amount of arsenic?"

"Of course not," my patient answered with some vehemence.

"Yet every day of your life you go to work and accept numerous small doses of emotional arsenic," I replied. John saw my point. Since then he has learned to declare.

John is a painter who shares a small painting business with a partner who sometimes tries to take advantage of him. In the past, John just endured or occasionally lost his temper and yelled. Now, when his partner says, "John, I'm just too hot; you finish the rest of this," John declares his own boundaries. "I'm sorry you're uncomfortable, Bill," he replies. "But I haven't got time to help you. You're on your own." Then he walks away, without debate, back to his own task. Bill can either continue painting or face the consequences of an angry customer and, eventually, if his behavior continues, the loss of a partnership.

The emotional results of John's declaring have been that John himself is no longer angry. He has even begun to like his partner once again. Bill has become more responsible, and his respect for John has returned to what it was before they almost ruined their relationship with their business partnership. Their mutual business dream was almost ruined by Bill's irresponsibility and John's unwillingness to declare.

Notice, too, that John did not tell Bill what he had to do. He just told him what he, John, would and would not do. He declared his own boundaries and by so doing placed Bill's responsibility for Bill back where it belonged, with Bill.

* * *

Simple as declaring is, and life transforming as it can be, its very simplicity can be deceiving. Many people think that such a simple concept cannot possibly work. Others think they understand the concept but don't. They think they are declaring, but they are not; then they are discouraged when what they have done doesn't work. There are several behaviors that may seem to be declarative but have nothing to do with declaring.

Declaring does not mean attacking. In the case of the two painters, telling Bill that he was a lazy bum or ordering him to go back to his painting would not have been declaring. The result, too, would have been the opposite of declaring, for Bill would have been angry, at best, or perhaps rebellious enough to quit. In return, John, who knew that his position was usually the fair one, would have been enraged. Declaring cuts anger; it does not cultivate anger. Declaring that builds anger rather than deflecting it is not true declaring.

A teenager with whom I have been working came in last week and said, "Aunt Sally was over for dinner and heard me tell a friend to shut up. When my aunt criticized me for using that term, I declared. I told her that, in view of what my friend had said, I didn't have a problem with my response. My aunt got angry at me and my mother grounded me. Declaring didn't work," she concluded. "It just made everyone angry at me."

For a moment I wondered if this was an exception to the guarantee that declaring reduces anger. Then, on impulse, I said, "Show me how you spoke to your aunt. Do it all over again, just as if I were your aunt."

Susan is dramatic, so I got the full impact. She came at me with her eyes blazing, established eye contact from just a few inches away, and screamed into my face, "I don't have a problem with what I said. She deserved it." Then, as if daring her aunt to disagree with her, she concluded by shouting, "Do you have a problem with that?"

She could have said, in a calm tone of voice, "After what my friend said to me, I don't feel bad about saying what I did." These words are somewhat better chosen. But actually her choice of words was not the major problem in her declaration. The menacing body movements and the angry, elevated voice constituted an attack, regardless of the choice of words.

Debating, too, is not declaring. "Why do you always have to interfere?" or "I wish you would try to understand me" could be opening statements for an argument between two people like Susan and her aunt. But they are not declarations.

Sometimes explanations and even debate are important in communication, but when someone like John the painter knows that what he feels is fair in a given situation, he doesn't need to debate or explain. To debate or to explain, when a declaration is more appropriate, arises from either ignorance of how to declare or from a need for the other person's approval.

In a related way, asking permission is another form of communication that fails to declare. You ask permission to borrow a hammer from your neighbor. You do not ask permission to get your own hammer back. You say nicely, but firmly, "I need the hammer returned by Saturday morning." Because it is not an attack or a demand, declaring can always be polite. It is always a reasonable statement of an individual's own boundaries.

* * *

For the Christian, declaring includes an added dimension of taking control of one's life in order to be under God's control. We cannot truly be under the control of God if that control belongs to other people. In its truest sense, declaring means stating God's boundaries for us. We are not our own, but we are bought with a price. As such, we belong under God's authority.

For the Christian, "Who controls my life?" is a major question. We can choose, even by default, to let others control us at whim. We can choose to take that control ourselves. Or we can transcend even that phase, choose to give the control of our lives to Jesus Christ, and then, under His direction, declare our boundaries to those with whom we deal. To do so is to become whole.

A young woman I met after speaking at a church told me that she walked into her living room one afternoon and saw her husband sitting on the living room floor with his eyes closed and hands folded, chanting, "Me! Me! Me!" over and over again.

When she asked him why he did it, he said it made him feel good. Taking control, if that's what he was doing, is not enough. For the Christian it means relinquishing that control back to God Himself. To do this is the opposite of the thinking of what has often been called the "me generation." To do this is the only way to truly find oneself.

The last stanza of an old hymn by George Matheson stands out in contrast to chanting "Me! Me! Me!" and is paradoxical in its truth.

> My will is not my own
>   Till thou hast made it Thine;
> If it would reach a monarch's throne
>   It must its crown resign;
> It only stands unbent
>   Amid the dashing strife,
> When on Thy bosom it has leant,
>   And found in Thee its life.[1]

* * *

To be under the authority of God and to live within His prescribed boundaries for our lives demand the opposite of passivity. They demand active declaring. Such confrontation, however, can still be gracious. An attractive Englishman began a conversation with me in a hotel lobby. The conversation ended with an invitation to spend the night in his room. I knew nothing about the man except that he had a wife and child in England and was looking forward to seeing them the next day. Indeed, he had talked about little else. Seizing upon that, I replied, "Wouldn't you feel better with your wife tomorrow if we just had another cup of coffee and went our separate ways?" He agreed, with almost a sense of relief. The declaration had not been an attack. It had been a simple statement of my God-directed boundaries.

There are times when such a proposition needs to be rebuffed more abrasively, yet often we can make our points most effectively with politeness and grace. Good manners should characterize those who call themselves Christians.

* * *

Politeness, or a commitment to "nice," however, can sometimes become an excuse to avoid declaring. Being nice to a child lying on the sidewalk screaming for candy is hardly a solution. Instead, walking away is an active declaration of "No."

In the same way the husband who sat down for dinner, saw that it was not to his liking, picked up the plate, and emptied it into the sink should not be rewarded with a new dinner. Peter's wife, who had been behaving as the loving spouse who catered to these tantrums, ended up in my office after enduring screaming fights and unreasonable demands. The marriage was almost destroyed, and the children were developing their own behavioral problems. Then she declared.

The next night after his wife saw me, Peter decided that his dinner wasn't hot enough, and so he dumped it in the sink. Quietly Martha told him that she was sorry he wasn't enjoying dinner and that there was more food in the refrigerator if he cared to prepare something else. When he ordered her to cook something else for him, she said she couldn't because she and the children were busy eating their dinners. Then she began to ask her children about their day. A few minutes later, to her amazement, Peter stomped back into the kitchen and made a cheese sandwich. Other problems in their marriage had to be worked out, but the tantrums over meals stopped.

In the context of this example, it is important to realize that even though declaring often changes the behavior of the person declared to, as in Peter's case, it doesn't always happen, and it can never be the main purpose of declaring. Declaring is to declare oneself, one's own boundaries, not those of someone else.

Martha had a difficult time declaring because it didn't seem nice; yet she found that screaming and yelling and tantrums aren't so nice either. "Nice" is not the same as godly. "Nice" can be a way you behave because you are too gutless to say "No." A commitment to niceness can make you say "Yes" to every demand and whim that comes along, so that you have no time or strength left to do what God really wants you to do. The end result of a commitment to niceness is burnout and anger. The culmination of a commitment to the will of God is peace.

We all know people who do good deeds because they can't say "No." They bring dinners to the church but never cook for their own families. They read to the blind but never to their own three-year-old child. Such people have lost control of their lives through a commitment to niceness rather than a commitment to the will of God. They have not learned that liberation can come through declaring.

* * *

To declare one's own boundaries, to take control of one's own life without having to change anyone else, is to experience freedom from bondage. When I was a high school teacher, I spent the first two years of my public school teaching trying to get my classes under control so that I could relax and go on. But it didn't work out that way. I couldn't force my students not to cheat. I couldn't make them study. I couldn't insist that they like English literature.

During my third year I discovered that, although I couldn't force change, I could declare my boundaries. When I said, "Don't you ever cheat in my classroom," I was daring them to cheat. Then I said, "I can't stop you from cheating, and I'm not even going to try. But if I do find that you have cheated, you will get two *F*'s for that paper rather than the one you would have gotten by simply failing." The situation stopped being me against them, and there seemed to be less of a problem with cheating. The same became true in other areas, like classroom behavior. I didn't wait for them to change. I changed.

* * *

Declaration takes practice. We all operate automatically in certain ways in our lives. Some of us automatically shout, become silent, debate, give in, or become nasty or nice. These automatic responses are like habits that have become part of our behavior over the years. Our friends are familiar with our sets of automatic responses, and they can sometimes guess how we will behave. I hear statements like, "John always becomes quiet in a crowd" and "I just know that Susan will scream at me when I cancel dinner." These statements are frequently based on the knowledge people have of our automatic responses.

For most people, to declare means not only to learn how it works in a practical way and to develop the art of declaring by trial and error but also to repeat the declaring enough times so that it becomes automatic in their lives. It means developing a new habit pattern, a new dimension of psychological and spiritual wholeness. This is where brain plasticity comes into play which adds another dimension to declaring boundaries.

With our relatively new knowledge of brain plasticity we now know that not only can we change habits, such as declaring instead of automatically giving in or debating, but that in so doing we actually change neural pathways. The brain itself changes. Dr. Pascual-Leone of Harvard Medical School likens the brain to "Play-Doh." He explains that the brain is very impressionable and that like "Play-Doh," which can be changed into various shapes, each time a shape is formed it will never be an exact replica of a previous shape. A ball will not be *exactly* like a previous ball. Because of our genetic makeup the brain remains somewhat consistent. Also by repetition the brain changes according to the pattern of that repetition rather than randomly.

Dr. Pascual-Leone explains this phenomena with the following illustration:

> The plastic brain is like a snowy hill in winter. Aspects of that hill—the slope, the rocks, the consistency of the snow—are, like our genes, a given. When we slide down on a sled, we can steer it and will end up at the bottom of the hill by following a path determined both by how we steer and the characteristics of the hill. ...

"But," Pascual-Leone says, "what will definitely happen the *second time* you take the slope down is that you will more likely than not find yourself somewhere or another that is related to the path you took the first time. It won't be exactly that path, but it will be closer to that one than any other. And if you spend your entire afternoon sledding down, walking up, sledding down, at the end you will have some paths that have been used a lot, some that have been used very little…

The mental "tracks" that get laid down can lead to habits, good or bad. If we develop poor posture, it becomes hard to correct. If we develop good habits, they too become solidified.[2]

Change occurs in the same way that the original habits were formed—by repetition. Changing habits can be difficult, especially if the habits are long standing. And there are studies which indicate possible ways to shorten the process. But essentially the stronger the focus becomes on the new habit the more quickly the new habit will replace the old.

According to Dr. Pascual-Leone, even imagining an act changes the material state of the brain. In truth, we become what we think—and see, and do, and hear. Hence the importance of the repeated biblical injunction to guard our affections, guard our thoughts, and to bring every thought into the captivity of our Lord. God who made us has always known what we are now learning about the brain, and He has taught us through His word to watch what we put into our minds and to focus on Him. Our times alone with God before we start the day; our words of encouragement to and from each other; the content of the books we read and the sermons we hear; the meaning of the hymns and songs we hear and sing: all these take on new importance. To a certain degree we choose who we become and we can choose to form new habits, new automatics.

The effect of the imagination on the brain does *not* justify the so-called "prosperity gospel." We do not become rich by thinking rich or become President of the United States by imagining that we have won an election. Within God's own boundaries we become better equipped to succeed in doing His will, however, when our thoughts are positive and our boundaries are declared.

For the Christian the bottom line is eventually about the will of God in us and through us. Some of the research on the brain can be a tool given to us by our Maker as we choose our way. Once again, in the words of the old hymn:

> My will is not my own
> > Till thou hast made it Thine...

Bible expositor F. B. Meyer expounds on the same thought when he says:

> Forget your feelings. Entrench yourself in YOUR WILL. Ask Jesus to purify and sanctify it by His Spirit, so that it may be true to Himself....
>
> *Will* to be free! *Will* to walk with God in stainless robes! *Will* to refuse the tempting bait! Will to deny flesh and to crucify self! *Will* because God is working in you to will. And you will find that if the WILL is present with you, the power to perform will also be forthcoming to your faith; and Jesus will make haste to achieve your complete deliverance. Lift up your heads and rejoice: your redemption draweth near.

Yes, and this will come to you, – that your will shall become more and more one with the will of God; so much so, that God will give you the keys of His kingdom, saying "Ask what ye *will*, and it shall be done unto you." And in proportion as the will of man is brought into unison and harmony with the will of God, there will be growing peace and growing power.[3]

Margaret, the head nurse in a high-stress medical setting, consulted me because she was committed to being nice and consequently could never confront anyone. Particularly troublesome to her was an abrasive supervisor who was her immediate superior and who was highly critical.

In our counseling sessions Margaret and I worked hard at developing her declaring skills. Her leadership qualities grew. She began to declare well, and yet she remained compassionate and open to change. Her co-workers respected her because they knew that if she had a complaint about one of them she would confront them constructively and privately. Yet every time the supervisor came by, at least a part of Margaret's day went down in defeat. Declaring was still not automatic in Margaret's life and certainly not automatic with her superior. The automatic comes with repetition which in turn works in part because of actual changes in brain activity. (See Chapter Four.)

One afternoon Margaret came to her counseling session radiant with enthusiasm. "I did it," she exclaimed as she sat down. "I declared to my supervisor without even thinking about what I was doing. It was automatic for the first time. I told her that I couldn't follow her orders unless she made sure I got those orders. I couldn't be blamed for not reading her mind. It all ended up a little strangely," Margaret added. "My supervisor just said that she would be sure to write the orders down early in the day, thanked me, and walked out. She was *less* angry than when I've said nothing!" Margaret had discovered the power of declaring, and for her the habit had become automatic.

* * *

Those we love and those in authority are probably the most difficult to declare to. After all, with them we have the most to lose. Mothers seem to be uniquely difficult to declare to because of the deep emotional bonds and because they are usually in positions of major influence in our lives. Yet, without the ability to declare to parents, husbands and wives, bosses at work, and other such authority figures, we never quite grow up. We are not fully whole individuals. Declaring is one means by which we grow up and claim our adulthood, not defensively as an adolescent but with the maturity that comes with issuing a statement that simply delineates one's own boundaries without requiring change from anyone else.

Charlene found herself getting upset after most phone calls with her mother. Her mother managed to make her feel guilty because they didn't see each other enough or because her mother felt that Charlene was spending too much time with her friends instead of with her mother. They disagreed, too, over the grandchildren and how they were being raised. "You know, dear, that son of yours is not going to amount to anything if you always say 'Yes' to him," the mother finally said. Charlene dissolved into tears.

When I talked to Charlene, I urged her to declare and save the relationship with her mother before they had a real fight and said things they would both always regret. With agony, she made the attempt. The next time her mother complained about her ten-year-old grandson, Charlene said, "I'm so glad that you're concerned, and I value your prayers, but we have to raise Jeff as we see fit."

Her mother replied, "Now dear, don't get upset. I'm just trying to help." In a statement that defused the whole debate, Charlene then answered, "I'm glad, but let's not talk about it anymore."

Charlene had declared her boundaries. The mother was a bit upset, but she soon got over it. For the first time in a long while, by the time the conversation ended, they had talked about other subjects, and both felt better. The mother was relieved of the obligation to keep making sure her daughter did the right thing, a habit that went back to Charlene's childhood. Charlene felt an adult relationship with her mother for the first time.

Her mother still advised at times, for old habits die slowly. But, now that advice at times was valued. After all, she did have insight from the experience of raising her own children. The mother gained status as a valued advisor, now that her daughter knew that she could always declare when she didn't agree.

Charlene would have to build her declaring into an automatic response by the process of repetition. Especially with her mother, she would have to redeclare her adult role from time to time. Rather than fighting back as a child, she would have to continue to choose to build an adult relationship with her mother.

Sometimes when the person we are declaring to is a lifelong authority figure, like a parent or just someone we highly respect, once we have declared our boundaries it is important to guard against going back to that authority figure for approval over our declaring. For example, you may declare that you cannot go to bed after ten on Sunday night. Then come Sunday you may feel the need to say to a spouse, "Do you mind if I don't stay up and watch the ten o'clock news with you?" Or, even more subtly, "I guess I'll go to bed now?" with a question mark at the end of the sentence which makes it more a bid for approval than it is a statement of fact. We do not need to get approval for declaring as long as we are declaring our own boundaries and no one else's.

* * *

The concept of choice is biblically based. Choosing God's way is the ultimate possibility of personal declaration. We belong to Him already by the right of Creation as well as Redemption. But God is a gentleman. He lets us choose. In the Old Testament, Joshua presented that choice very articulately. To his challenge to the people, "...Decide today whom you will obey," Joshua's own answer was: "But as for me and my family, we will serve the Lord" (Josh. 24:15 TLB).

A plaque, made in the mid-nineteenth century in Sweden and given to my maternal grandparents for their wedding, states Joshua's personal response in Swedish and hangs in my living room as a declaration of the choice of my family. It is a declaration of this household and those from it who have gone on before.

To declare is an important tool to be learned in the safety zone of the counseling relationship. It is a tool that helps to enable the building of bigger dreams than we ever thought possible. It helps to make dream builders of dream bashers, and it protects dream builders from dream bashers. Above all, it helps us choose God's way and clears away the debris of indecision and fearfulness with renewed conviction and determination.

The result? Wholeness! C. S. Lewis describes that as well as anyone I've read:

> Imagine yourself as a living house. God comes in to rebuild that house. At first, perhaps, you can understand what he is doing. He is getting the drains right and stopping the leaks in the roof and so on: you knew that those jobs needed doing and so you are not surprised. But presently he starts knocking the house about in a way that hurts abominably and does not seem to make sense. What on earth is he up to? The explanation is that he is building quite a different

house from the one you thought of – throwing out a new wing here, putting on an extra floor there, running up towers, making courtyards. You thought you were going to be made into a decent little cottage: but he is building a palace. He intends to come and live in it himself.[4]

How well I understand that nervous breaking down from which you have suffered. Let it be a warning. There is a limit you should not attempt to pass in exhausting labors. It is not easy to fix it, but experience shows pretty clearly where it is. I have been beyond it at times, when all the foundations of life seemed gone. I cannot express what that means, and hope you will never know. Most people have no conception how thin the foundations are which keep them above the abyss, where the interests of life exist no more. I tell you this, for you need to be warned. Learn to say "No" to invitations or calls to labour which destroy the power to labour and the possibility of service.

– Grattan Guinness

Eight

Playing Cheetah

It was a misty, overcast day. Here and there dense black clouds threatened to turn the soft drizzle into torrents of rain. As if in response to the uncertain atmosphere, traffic on one of the most crowded of all California freeways moved more slowly and less predictably than ever. It was, in general, a good day to stay home! Yet with a sense of illogical logic that such was the pathway to tranquility, my daughter and I battled the elements and the Los Angeles freeways to meet a friend for tea. We had planned this escape for a week; in recent days, the pressures of life had been unusually heavy. Now, no inconvenience of weather, distance, or traffic jams was going to stop us from a much-needed break.

As we drove off the freeway and down the coast toward the hotel where we were to meet our friend, even the ocean appeared gray. Yet as we approached the hotel and watched the waves washing up over the beach below, once again, as always, the sea began to have its calming effect on me.

To complete the scene, the hotel lobby, with its great bowls of flowers and its crackling fireplace inside, added a contrast of cheerfulness to the gray skies and the turbulent sea outside, a contrast I have always found to be enormously uplifting. The knot in my stomach relaxed, and I no longer felt in a hurry. The safety zone of afternoon tea with good friends in a relaxing atmosphere was beginning to have its positive effect.

As we waited to be seated, a lady in front of us turned to her friend and said, "This morning I felt in such turmoil I knew that if I didn't plan this I wasn't going to make it." Her friend smiled understandingly and agreed that she, too, had known such days.

The friend we came to meet was late. She was the only one of us who didn't have the day off, and so she was rushing to get away from work as early as possible. After some time went by in that pre-cell phone era, a telephone message was relayed to us explaining that she was late but on her way.

Enjoying the luxury of a whole day off, I felt a twinge of guilt. If you rush too much to get to a safety zone, the safety zone can become just another high wire, another demand that adds to rather than detracts from the demands of life. I thought that perhaps I should call my friend and tell her that we understood if she couldn't make it, but I didn't have her work number with me. So we waited.

We finally sat down and let our tea steep while we continued to wait. I looked out the window at the sea once again, and I felt the tranquility of the scene: the sea outside, the warmth inside, and the serenity of just doing nothing. Steeping tea cannot be hurried. It takes its time, no matter what the immediacy of the situation. Maybe that's part of what makes taking tea have such great potential for providing a safety zone. It slows us down. It forces either contemplation or conversation.

Then I looked across the room and saw my friend approaching. "This is just what I need," she commented, with the conspiratorial smile of one who has escaped in spite of many obstacles. "I'm so glad I didn't give up on coming," she said; and I was glad I hadn't called and discouraged her. The three of us had all needed a safety zone that provided a break from the everyday pressure. We didn't need, nor could we take, a vacation in the south of France, but we did need that minibreak that can make, in a cumulative way, the difference between going on and burning out. If burnout can come in small increments, so can relief be provided by many small occasions of relief.

* * *

Burnout is the current buzzword that simply reiterates a condition that has always been a problem for those who have too much to do and too little time in which to do it. In many of our lives, dealing with burnout is a dimension of wholeness which we fail to notice. The old truism that if you want something done right, find someone who's busy has always been accurate. Out of this truth can come the basis for burnout.

Some of us have tired of the word *burnout*, partly because the word has become so overused that it has come to mean everything from overwork to laziness and boredom. I have had people consult me after two days on a job complaining of burnout. Now, it is possible to feel that you have the wrong job after two days of work, but it is not possible to be truly burned out! Similarly, students who never study but feel burned out at school may have a problem with school but not with burnout.

High-wire living, walking on water, and *doing it all* are more apt descriptions to me of what is commonly called *burnout.* Whatever we call it, however, none of us is equipped to cope with the condition of top-speed living in the fast lane. Even in a society where an ulcer is a badge of executive success and how far you travel and how late you work are sometimes confused with efficiency, none of us can do it all. We must make tough decisions. We must choose priorities.

* * *

Sometimes the decisions are agonizing and very personal. A number of years ago I came very close to adopting a small child. The further I got in the paperwork, the more I slowed down. Then I realized that *for me,* with the absorption I had in my work, I could not add a small child to my life. If I did, my work would suffer or the child would lack nurturing.

A few years ago a man I knew distantly intrigued me. He seemed to be able to do it all at a time when I had become completely convinced that sensible living was the only long-range way to plan one's life. He was raising a large family, had a high-powered career, conducted seminars on his days off, and was very active in a large church. Secretly I envied his endurance and was tempted to think that if I tried a little harder maybe I could walk on water too. Fortunately, I didn't change my life-style because of him. Two years later, he had a heart attack and developed a chronic disease that will slow him down for the rest of his life. He just *looked* as if he could walk on water. He couldn't; none of us can.

Burnout, trying to walk on water as a way of life, doesn't work for anyone. Students who stay up all night studying for tests usually don't do as well in their classes as students who consistently study and get proper sleep. My writing goes better when I plan it out over a period of months and don't try to do it all at one time. The quality of my work improves, and the stress on my body is incredibly reduced. In the long run we accomplish more, both in quantity and in quality, by steadiness and pacing, and certainly we last longer.

In a striking statement about our inability to do it all, Samuel Rutherford once wrote, "There is but a certain quality of spiritual force in any man. Spread it over a broad surface, the stream is shallow and languid; narrow the channel and it becomes a driving force." In connection with this statement, missionary Amy Carmichael added, "We must learn to plough deep rather than wide. Only God can plough both deep and wide."[1] Indeed, Jesus Christ, God-Man, is the only One who has ever walked on water. Walking on water is not the province of mortal man.

* * *

High-wire living not only affects our work adversely, but also can damage our relationships with other people. Friends who commit to accommodating everyone's needs and try to do it all fail at some point out of sheer exhaustion and, in spite of all their efforts, in the end disappoint people because of that failure.

I hear people make statements like "Call me any hour of the night if you need me." I cringe inside, not because I doubt the value of being available for someone who is in a real state of crisis, but because I hear these same people say this to almost everyone they talk to. Then, if too many people take them up on their offer, they back off, usually abruptly and without warning. The end result is that through their overextension they end up hurting the people they most wanted to help, while they themselves feel guilty and a bit resentful over what they now view as "being used."

The marital relationship is probably the most sensitive, intimate human relationship in this world. As such it is also the human relationship most vulnerable to hurt and most able to give joy. Those who try to have it all by making their spouses do more than they can manage can very easily end up destroying their marriages.

Repeatedly in my counseling office I see couples in which the wife wants the husband to get out and make more money, and at the same time she wants him to do more household tasks and spend more time with their children. The man ends up in my office defensive and angry because he's tried to do it all and it wasn't enough.

In a similar way, men who want their wives to work full-time often expect them to continue to maintain all the household tasks and to assume full care of the children. One woman I know just quit her job. Her husband had forced her into a job she hadn't even wanted and then refused to give up his three nights of volleyball each week in order to baby-sit while she worked. He still can't figure out why she "won't do her share."

* * *

People who try to walk on water generally drown; while they sink, many others stand by and criticize or wonder what's wrong with the person. Only a few are perceptive enough to see that this person isn't weak but just doing too much. By the time he or she reaches my counseling office, the would-be water-walker has thoroughly bought into the idea of being "weak" and is making statements like "If I were stronger, I could have done this" or, depending on their orientation, "If I were a better Christian, I wouldn't be here." They feel as though they did all they could do and more, and it wasn't enough. Their self-images are down, their bodies are sick, and they don't feel up to trying harder. To declare their boundaries is not in their vocabulary, and so they feel like hopeless failures.

It becomes the obligation of counseling to help people set realistic boundaries while they learn to declare those boundaries to others. In her speech at the Wellesley commencement ceremonies in 1990, First Lady Barbara Bush exhorted the graduates to choose their priorities in life carefully. If we can't do it all, we can at least make wise choices. Mrs. Bush warned, "At the end of your life, you will never regret not having passed one more test, not winning one more verdict, or not closing one more deal. You will regret time not spent with a husband, a child, a friend or a parent...."

Sometimes our families want fewer things from us: smaller houses, cheaper clothes, and more modest forms of entertainment. Sometimes those we love most just want more of us and our time rather than the material extras we can give them by working two jobs. A young child who had been rescued from a series of abusive situations was at last living safely with his father. Their house was located in a modest neighborhood. They lived in financially tight circumstances, but each member of the family was surrounded by much love. Coming home late one night, as the car turned the corner on their street, the child murmured sleepily, "Daddy, I just love this street." He hadn't noticed that the houses were old and needed painting or that the sidewalks were cracked. He didn't seem to mind sharing his room with two brothers. He just knew that on this street he was loved, and love made the street beautiful to him.

* * *

To a limited extent, high-wire living has some legitimate function, and it is not always neurotically motivated. A crisis or an emergency can warrant the use of a high-wire response. The response is not meant to be long-range, however. A forest fire, for example, requires everyone who is nearby to do anything possible *until* added help arrives. On the domestic front, a woman who is a single parent and who goes to an office at nine every morning may find that she needs to spend an occasional sleepless night with a sick child. If the illness extends itself over a period of time, she cannot continue the nightly vigil as well as her job. At this point she will need to get off the high wire by finding someone to help with the child or by taking a few days off work.

Accidents, illnesses, earthquakes, and floods – as well as smaller occurrences, like stopped-up drains, family arguments, complaints from neighbors, and calls from a child's teacher – comprise the types of extraordinary events that require a response that is not planned into our ordinary daily schedule. However, if we are living well-planned lives with time out for rest and recreation, the emergencies, both small and large, will not overwhelm as much. We will have a reserve we can use to meet them. If we are already overwhelmed and living close to the edge of our emotional and physical resources on a daily basis, however, these added pressures will seem insurmountable. Even a broken faucet will become too much to cope with.

* * *

Normal life itself, without any emergencies, has a limited high-wire quality scattered throughout. Any job worth doing intensifies our efforts at certain points. When I write, for example, I rarely stay passive. My intensity builds to the point where my topic consumes me. The subject matter is, at that moment, the most important thing in the world to me. Without that, my writing becomes passive and flat.

Passion makes all of us better at what we are doing, whether we are planning a school play, baking bread, drawing up plans for a new house, performing surgery, or selling cars. Depending on the amount of intensity involved, however, times of rest and recreation must punctuate the activity. How effectively we alternate these rest periods with the work periods will determine whether burnout occurs. Jobs ordinarily have break periods and paid vacations for this reason.

The danger starts when we begin to work through lunch, skip breaks, or landscape our yards and take classes during our vacation times. Sometimes exceptions can be made. For someone who works at an accounting firm most of the year, painting the house during a vacation can be a useful change, as long as it does not become a pattern for every vacation. Working late to meet a deadline is legitimate, as long as the additional hours are the exception rather than the rule.

* * *

The life-style of the cheetah is very instructive to those of us who tend to try to do it all. In the opinion of most experts, the cheetah is the fastest animal on earth. At its peak it can run up to seventy miles an hour. It is a magnificent sight to watch the cheetah run at top speed, flexing its powerful muscles as it seems to glide over the land and barely touch the ground. Its speed enables the cheetah to be a remarkable hunter. Yet it can maintain that speed for only a short time. Then it stops totally in order to regain the strength to run seventy miles an hour once again.

Like the cheetah, if we run seventy miles an hour, we must stop every now and then. The trouble with many of us is that we think we can continue running at seventy miles an hour without ever stopping. Then, when we fall, we feel as though we are weak, as though we have failed. The problem was that we played cheetah by rushing at top speed, but we didn't play cheetah when it was time to stop for a while. If you are going to run like a cheetah, you have to stop like a cheetah.

I once had a small sheltie with a big-dog personality. Keeping vigil over the apartment where I live was his full-time task. He expended a prodigious amount of energy racing from window to window, watching those who came and went, and barking fiercely at intruders. His intense life-style competed with the cheetah's seventy-miles-per-hour life-style. He provided a constant example to me of high-wire intensity personified.

Yet, like the cheetah, he could shut down from high speed to complete immobility in a matter of seconds. When he slept, his repose was so deep that you had to touch him or shout to wake him up. Horace ran like a cheetah, but he also stopped like a cheetah. In this way he constantly renewed his energy.

* * *

Some of us work quickly by nature. We love our work and we tend to want to keep going at it. We, more than anyone else, need to learn to play cheetah. Churchill once wrote quite succinctly of those who have heavy responsibilities and of their need for relief: "Change is the master key."[2] We could add, change is a master key to becoming whole. On the other hand, overextension destroys wholeness.

Consistent with that thought, people who work inside may need to go outside for recreation. Teachers may not want to teach Sunday school. Housepainters will not find rest by painting their own houses on weekends. They may have to do it now and then, but it will be work for them, not recreation.

Thus, one person's relaxation may be another person's work. In marriage counseling I find that a big problem between spouses is their lack of perception of the other's needs at the end of a day. On the one hand, the person who comes home from an office building often wants quiet and rest. Providing a forty-five-minute period of isolation from any demands, including those of the children, or becoming a listener for that person will usually solve the problem.

On the other hand, the person who has been at home all day, cleaning, cooking, and talking to three-year-old minds, needs companionship and even excitement. Watching a movie after the children are in bed, a late-night talk over cups of hot chocolate, or occasionally hiring a baby-sitter for an evening out will generally help to alleviate the tensions of the day for that person. However, rather than giving each other what they need by a process of give-and-take, the tendency is to argue instead. Then both partners feel misunderstood and alone.

Once they see that the other person's needs are different from their own, much progress can be made in counseling couples who have this type of problem. Furthermore, if learning to express such needs and becoming perceptive to a spouse's changing needs are the result of spending time in the safety zone of counseling, then, as children grow older and perhaps both spouses go out to work, the couple will be able to perceive on their own the resultant changes in their needs and think of ways to meet their new needs.

Therefore, playing cheetah is not only planning our lives realistically and resting physically. Playing cheetah is also finding activities that provide change from our normal routine. It is important to know ourselves. A forest ranger might find relaxation in city life; someone living in the middle of Manhattan might need a lake or a mountain range.

* * *

Winston Churchill also provides valuable insight on the different needs of those who like their work and those who just do their jobs routinely. Those who enjoy what they are doing are, according to Churchill, "Fortune's favoured children.... For them the working hours are never long enough. Each day is a holiday, and ordinary holidays when they come are grudged as enforced interruptions in an absorbing vocation." Although both groups need to play cheetah, and both need change and relaxation, "It may well be that those whose work is their pleasure are those who most need the means of banishing it at intervals from their minds."[3] It is difficult to break away from an absorbing task.

Coming from a different time than Churchill, and certainly more entrenched in the Puritan work ethic, the famous preacher Charles Spurgeon wrote with amazing balance on the subject of refurbishment after labor. In comparing such needs with the animal world, he cautioned that even animals eat and lie down after their activity. Physical rest, too, is an important dimension of good mental health. Once again the body, mind, and spirit work together. Where Churchill stresses change, Spurgeon stresses quietness and meditation upon God, but both saw the need for balancing work with rest. Both saw the need for diversion.

In contrast to the feelings of failure that arise from burnout, Spurgeon promises, "You will return to your business in a better spirit; you may expect (other things being equal) to earn more that day, than you ever earned before, by the painful system of uninterrupted drudgery; for the diversion of thought will rest, string up, and brace your nerves, and enable you to do more work, and do it better too."[4]

* * *

Many delusions are connected with trying to do it all. When I was a college student, I took a full load at the university and a partial load at a theological seminary – at the same time! I also taught Sunday school, dated several times a week, and held part-time jobs on campus. To top it off, I graduated early. I did all this with the help of several delusions, the major one being that if it looked okay on paper it would work. I arranged my classes at UCLA for Monday, Wednesday, and Friday. I went to seminary on Tuesday and Thursday. Work fit in between classes during what I called "extra" time. Church and dating were necessary recreation, I reasoned. However, the plan didn't work. I made it through school, but I ran down my physical resources in the process. I was, in the best definition of the term, *burned out*. At the root of my problems was the attitude that if it looked good written on a schedule it would work.

One problem with my schedule was that it didn't allow enough time for rest. It counted activities like teaching children as recreation, when in actuality they were work. It didn't allow for traffic jams, bouts of flu, telephone calls, cooking, extra academic assignments, favors for friends, or even just time to *be*.

For me, at least, this trying to walk on water also got confused with what looked like the will of God. After all, what better way could an eighteen-year-old use her time than by going to Bible seminary and teaching Sunday school? I hadn't learned what many people I counsel never learn: to choose between the good and the good. It is easy to clear our lives of so-called bad things; it's much harder to say "No" to the good.

Entering into this way of thinking is what psychologist Rollo May has called the Messiah Complex. Good people often feel that a need constitutes an obligation. If there is a legitimate need, they must meet it. Underneath this mentality is the idea that if I don't do it, nobody else will. Good people need to confront the needs around them by asking, "Is this a need I am meant to meet?" We need more of that helping attitude in this world. Indeed, such an attitude is a basic Christian characteristic. However, beware of assuming that if there is a need *you* must meet it. As Christians we must be led more specifically than that.

The late J. B. Phillips, a noted Bible translator, was a good example of a man tortured by what appears to be, at least in part, burnout. As I read of his life, a flashing red light came on when I learned that for a long time Dr. Phillips took on every request for speaking as a leading from God. The need constituted a call from God. The result was burnout from which he never really recovered.

* * *

Motives for water-walking are numerous. For some of us, high-wire living has an appeal that simply fits our personalities and perhaps goes back as far as our childhood years. There is so much to do and so little time to do it. One day when I was looking through the slips of paper and clippings my mother had kept in her well-worn Bible, I found one on which my mother had written, "Elizabeth said today (at age four), 'I'm too busy to sleep.'" Reading that brief note reinforced my conviction that slowing down has always been a struggle for me. At the same time, learning to pace my life has been one of my greatest personal victories.

Sometimes, too, as in the example of Dr. Phillips, the needs that a certain person can uniquely fill seem so pressing. I'm sure that in times of national crisis or catastrophic disaster, people with outstanding, rare talents face a constant threat of burnout.

Trying to walk on water is a problem that builds upon so many seemingly unrelated issues. When it is based on obvious factors, like temperament or unique, crisis-type needs that press in from outside, even then, no matter how much we enjoy what we are doing, and no matter how genuine and even worthwhile the demands of the crisis, eventually we must play cheetah and stop. Walking on water cannot become a life-style if we are going to survive.

* * *

On a more neurotic level, certain people just can't say "No," even when they want to. For others, an overly busy schedule seems to indicate success or being needed. For them, burnout becomes a status symbol. For these people, high-wire living relates, at least partially, to low self-esteem and problems with declaring, since secure people are more likely to be realistic about their capacities and able to declare their boundaries once they know how.

Burnout relates also to the spiritual dimension of our being in the sense that many people who burn out have the false belief that they are burning out for God. Paradoxically, rather than automatically viewing God as a motivating force in burnout, we often need divine guidance to discern when to say "No." Then it may take special divine strength to utter the word "No."

Neurotic guilt is a very real issue in burnout, and many people who seek counseling relate experiences of over-committing simply because they did not want to deal with guilt feelings. Guilt is often confused with spiritual issues because of a failure to differentiate between neurotic and realistic guilt. When I feel guilty because I have done something wrong, I need forgiveness. Then I need to change my behavior so that I do not make the same mistake again. In contrast, neurotic guilt is not based on actual wrongdoing but on what is imagined. For those who experience a sense of neurotic guilt, saying "No" can be a painful experience because it starts the recordings playing: *If I were a stronger person I could do this*, or *How can I say "No" when there is no one else to meet the need?* or just *What if my friends don't like me because I've said "No"?*

For many, trying to do it all is simply a way of avoiding the space and quietness of stopping. For them, burnout is the classic symptom of the disease of our time, loneliness. Loneliness, in turn, connects with other factors that affect burnout, such as self-esteem and spiritual wholeness. The best antidotes for loneliness are to like ourselves enough to enjoy being alone and to have a personal relationship with God.

From the point of view of a counselor, the sad part about water-walkers is that they always do too much and feel strung out and tired, yet they never feel they do enough. To do so much and then to fail is the fate of water walking. To play cheetah is, in simple language, the cure.

Then comes the most Christian challenge of all: to do good just for the sake of doing good. It is easy to feed the poor whenever a neurotic need to save the world drives us to it; it's harder when we do it only because it's the right thing to do. It's easy to sit up half the night on the phone with a distressed person when having that person call us with a problem makes us feel needed. But when we already feel needed, and someone reaches out to us to talk at an inconvenient time, it takes the love of God to extend ourselves.

* * *

Therefore, although a low self-image drives a great many people to contradictory and often destructive behavior, having good mental health is an awesome responsibility. For wholeness expands the opportunity for choice, whereas fragmentation limits personal choice. I see children, for example, who react in very diverse ways when they feel neglected by their parents. One child may go on a high wire, overachieve in school, and compete to almost impossible extremes in sports just to please his parents. When the parents don't even notice his achievements, the child may become bitter or hopeless, or he may decide that he'll build a life for himself in spite of his parents' neglect.

Another child in the same family may react to the neglect with clear-cut anger: acts of violence, neighborhood vandalism, or membership in a gang where he *does* feel important. Still a third child in the same family may become withdrawn and daydream a lot, or he may become depressed and even suicidal.

How a given child responds to neglect depends on that child's position in the family, how the child perceives the neglect, and personal temperament, as well as outside factors such as a concerned schoolteacher or a talent for something like art combined with the opportunity to develop that talent.

All the behaviors produced in such a family, however, have one root cause: feelings of low self-worth resulting from parental neglect. Trying to walk on water in order to compensate is only one of the possible symptoms.

In contrast, good mental health tends to take away the neurotic need to prove ourselves, to take revenge for past wrongs, or to feel constantly guilty even when any realistic reason for guilt is removed. Wholeness enables free choice, and with free choice comes the obligation to do right.

Choosing to do good rather than being driven to it means the difference between a life lived in chaos and a life lived with order and control. Furthermore, morality that arises from choice rather than bondage receives greater reward from God. After all, there's not much virtue involved in doing something just because you can't say "No."

A colleague once told me of a patient he had been seeing who had lived for years on high wires. His health ran down and he had finally sought professional help. After several months of therapy, one morning the man suddenly commented on the beauty of a red geranium that was blooming outside the doctor's office. "It's always been there," my friend replied. "You've just never noticed it." Seeing the red geranium was the first indication the patient gave of real progress toward normal living. For the first time in years, the man had literally stopped long enough to smell the flowers.

In a similar situation, after weeks of therapy, I had someone pause as they left my office. "Has that fireplace always been there?" they asked. When I replied "Yes" they barely believed me. They were becoming more whole.

* * *

Even if we are not actually living on a high wire, sometimes we don't realize how fast we have been going. My encounter with the ocean following the surgery previously referred to helped me put my life into perspective. I was physically weak and in some pain. Worst of all for me, my thinking was foggy from the anesthesia and pain medication. I had planned to use this time of recuperation for thinking about book ideas and organizing my current writing schedule. If I couldn't see my patients, I had naively assumed, with the ignorance of one who has never before had major surgery, I could at least have more time to write and think about writing. It didn't work that way, and for the first time in a long while I had to be content with doing nothing.

Three days after surgery I slowly put a day's effort into walking outside and up some stairs at my motel to a table surrounded by lawn chairs. Exhausted by the exertion, I relaxed into one of the chairs and looked out at the ocean in front of me. This time the sea was bright blue and the sky was sunny. A couple of sailboats drifted by slowly. The moderately high waves, tipped with foam, came in toward me and then disappeared from my view under the grassy cliffs. The cycle repeated itself with a kind of hypnotic monotony. Farther out, the sea looked blue and calm, stretching back into a sky that seemed to come down to meet it. Overhead, the sea gulls flew back and forth, like choreographed beings used as stage props to enhance the beauty of the sea with its painted ships and to add their sounds in a kind of symphony with the waves.

As I watched the scene, I realized how long it had been since I had really *seen* the sea. I thought I had watched it. Certainly it had uplifted me often. However, not for years had I just sat quietly and absorbed its beauty – not looking for inspiration, not looking for anything really. As I slowly made my way back down the steps toward my room, I realized that the sight of that blue ocean, always there, always the same, had quieted my restlessness.

I tried to use the time of my illness for a time of productivity, and I found that instead I had been forced to play cheetah and stop altogether. Yet, strangely enough, the time had not been wasted at all. I had seen the majesty of the sea and had reflected on the One under whose control we all remain. When once again I returned to my work, it was with a sense of renewal that I had not known in a long time.

The pessimist resembles a man who observes with fear and sadness that his wall calendar, from which he daily tears a sheet, grows thinner with each passing day. On the other hand, the person who attacks the problems of life actively is like a man who removes each successive leaf from his calendar and files it neatly and carefully away with its predecessors, after first having jotted down a few diary notes on the back. He can reflect with joy on all the richness set down in these notes, on all the life he has already lived to the full. What will it matter to him if he notices that he is growing old? Has he any reason to envy the young people he sees, or wax nostalgic over his own lost youth? What reasons has he to envy a young person? For the possibilities open to a young person, the future that is in store for him? "No, thank you," he will think. "Instead of possibilities, I have realities in my past, not only the reality of work done and of love loved, but of sufferings bravely suffered. These sufferings are the things of which I am most proud, though these are things which cannot inspire envy."

– Viktor E. Frankl

NINE

SPIRIT POWER

M r. Sam Eddie," the receptionist called out into the hospital waiting room. The large waiting area was full of people waiting to have their blood drawn, hopefully soon so that they could go home.

An elderly man across from me rose to his feet with that look of hesitancy that so often accompanies a feeling of not being sure whether your name or that of someone else was called.

"Mr. Sam Eddie?" the receptionist inquired of the man as he approached her.

"Oh no," he mumbled. "I'm Freddie Brown."

The receptionist smiled with that patronizing look people sometimes get around the elderly when they conclude that age has made a person incompetent. Assuming the tone of voice and the facial expression of one speaking to a small child, she replied, "Don't worry. We'll get to you soon."

With a look of awkward embarrassment, Mr. Freddie Brown returned to his seat and sat down. He rubbed his face nervously and glanced quickly around to see how many people had observed his faux pas.

Not long afterwards the receptionist called out another name. "Melissa Smith, please come to the desk."

No one moved. To one side of the room two teenage girls sat chatting. After the second call for Melissa Smith, one girl nudged the other and said laughingly, "Pay attention, that's you!" The receptionist smiled, and no one turned to look.

A man in his eighties wasn't sure that it was his name that was called. A teenager didn't even hear her name or any other name called! In terms of confusion or lack of accuracy of hearing, the teenager was the worst offender. The assumption of senility for the older man arose from the apparent age of the individual, not from the symptoms he presented.

* * *

It's a principle of living that we each have a lot to do with what other people become, for they tend to become what we expect them to become. In a rough paraphrase of Goethe: if we treat people as if they are already what they should become, we help them to become it. In no two periods of life is this concept more aptly portrayed than in childhood and again in old age. I have seen children denigrated, with the result that they grew up feeling worthless. Conversely, I have seen children praised and encouraged until they actually achieved far more than anyone ever thought possible.

A little boy who had been in many foster homes was finally adopted. His first teacher in the school near his new home praised him almost too much, I thought. Yet because of her encouragement, he worked hard in her class and started to catch up on the years of school he had lost. Then his adopted family moved and he started at a new school. "You're going to end up in jail someday," the teacher shouted at him in anger when the child disturbed her class for the third time in one day. After a few similar statements, his behavior grew steadily worse. One day he stole from a grocery store. His comment to me afterwards was: "I might as well steal; that's what everyone expects me to do!"

At least children can look forward to the day when they will have more complete control of their destinies and when their value to society will exceed that of tax deductions for their parents. For the elderly, there is no such hope. If their present is dismal, their hope for the future is darker still. Rather than old age being a time of honor, as in the older Chinese culture, or a time of spiritual leadership and even reward, which is part of the Judeo-Christian heritage, age has become to our present society the disease of our time. We predestine ourselves and others to a dread of old age, and in some kind of self-fulfilling prophecy it truly becomes, in many instances, a terrible time.

* * *

Certain aspects of aging can be dreadful. Brittle bones, poverty, loss of memory, and helplessness are at times realistic expectations. For those who are the relatives or friends of the elderly person thus afflicted, it is often difficult to know what to do. It is important to realize, however, that our own attitudes toward aging and the aged tend to influence how well the elderly handle their lives. As often as not, negative expectations of the elderly do them as much harm as the actual afflictions themselves. Furthermore, the kinds of perceptions we have regarding old age will help to determine not only our treatment of the elderly but also our own gradual but inevitable aging process.

When my mother died of injuries sustained in a car accident, she was eighty years old. For eleven days after the accident, she fought to live. At the scene of the accident, she was clearer than anyone else regarding the practical details, such as who was in the car and where they lived. For seven years after the death of my father, she had lived in their house by herself. She gardened, baked, took care of two dogs, painted some of her best work, and was, in general, an active participant in life. Above all, she was fun. She could always be ready at a moment's notice to go out for a late supper or to take a ride by the ocean.

Yet one of the doctors who didn't know her and, indeed, had never met her before the surgery that followed the accident – and who ironically was elderly and white-haired himself – greeted me with the question, "Which convalescent home was she in?"

When I replied that she had never been in a convalescent home, the doctor responded, "Anyone who is eighty should be in a convalescent home!"

His opinion is a perfect illustration of the idiotic preconceptions that sometimes plague the elderly. Unfortunately, when the elderly themselves hear such statements, they sometimes begin to feel that maybe, after all, they are useless. They can begin to become what they hear others saying about them.

Furthermore, for those who deal with aging loved ones or help others work with them, it is important to clarify within our own minds our view of the meaning of old age.

* * *

After centuries of seeking the fountain of youth, we have now doubled our life expectancy. But what is the value of these added years? Sorting out our values on aging, including our own aging, can be a function of the safety zone of counseling. If we view old age as throwaway years, we make it hard to find meaning in those years, and we make it very difficult for those who are caretakers of the aged. Time so spent will seem wasted and difficult.

It had been an unusual day in my office. After years of listening to people, not many problems shock or upset me in the sense that they profoundly disturb my personal life. In my office I am totally involved in my patients' problems, but when I leave that office, I cut the worries and concerns of that day. This day was different.

The child I had seen was only seven, but she had endured months of brutal sexual molestation from an uncle who seemed, to all outward appearances, totally normal. Something like this is always hard to deal with emotionally. Still, I have seen numbers of children who have been either physically abused or sexually molested. Some have been much younger than seven. Perhaps it was the frequency of the acts against this child that horrified me; perhaps it was the fact that for so long no one had listened to her or defended her that bothered me so much. Perhaps it was the attitude of the uncle, who regretted what he had done but, by his own admission, would have gone out and done the same thing again if it had been possible. Perhaps it was the volume of details I heard, not only from the child, who was hesitant, but also from the uncle himself, who seemed unable to resist enjoying his recital of lurid details.

I came home that night feeling physically sick to my stomach. It was one of those times when I felt that only the purity of God Himself could cleanse me from what I had heard and help me put it from my mind. I felt alone, and so I picked up the phone and called a friend, the mother of a childhood schoolmate of mine.

My friend is elderly. She is not in wonderful health. She is a godly woman who has probably not ever heard anything quite like what I heard in my office that day. Nevertheless, I knew she would understand, and she did. As we talked, I felt that sense of godly authority from her that is so characteristic of those who have walked with God for many years. The nausea left, and I was able to cut the mental recordings and commit the child to God.

I was reminded again of the challenges in the New Testament for older women to counsel those who are younger. I thought, too, of the verses that warn against one Christian saying to another, in essence, "I don't need you." We all need each other, the aged and the young alike.

> From childhood I am inspired with wonder;
> From adolescence I am challenged to question
> and search;
> From adulthood I am inspired by ambition and
> work;
> From old age, I discover reward, contemplation
> and sharing.

By sharing between different age groups, those who are older retain the good of the age they have outgrown while those who are younger share the benefits of those who are ahead of them in time. Those who are not yet aged cannot afford to say to the aged, "I don't need you." We need them very much, and they need us.

* * *

In our society retirement often becomes a signpost marking the end of productivity and the beginning of the great slide downhill toward death. The gift of a watch at that time is appropriate as a symbol of the last countdown. Often the retiree tries to deny the inevitable, for a while at least, by a burst of activity; others slump into a hopeless resignation to the inevitable from which they never completely recover.

Although old age marks the latter end of life, that fact does not contradict the equal truth that old age can be a time of great meaning. Those years are not throwaway years. Otherwise God, who holds all time in His hands, would certainly remove all old people from the earth, for He does not leave any of us here without a purpose. Indeed, in the thoughts of the psalmist, God has scheduled each day of our lives before we begin to breathe. (Psalm 139) Each day has value.

Charles Spurgeon has aptly stated, "Old age is a time of peculiar memories, of peculiar hopes, of peculiar solicitudes, of peculiar blessedness, and of peculiar duties."[1] Arguing against those who view aging as a time of defeat, General Douglas MacArthur is quoted as saying:

> People grow old only by deserting their ideals. . . .
> Years may wrinkle the skin, but to give up interest
> wrinkles the soul. . . . You are as young as your
> faith, as old as your doubt; as young as your self-

confidence, as old as your fear; as young as your
hope, as old as your despair. In the central place
of every heart there is a recording chamber; so
long as it receives messages of beauty, hope,
cheer and courage, so long are you young.
When…your heart is covered with the snows
of pessimism and the ice of cynicism, then and
only then are you grown old.[2]

The general would have agreed, I believe, that we can measure
our age by the recorded mental messages we play.

* * *

As we begin to see those we love grow older and at times become
increasingly helpless, however, it is natural to question the value
of life at that point. We read the words of English poet Robert
Browning, "The best is yet to be," and we wonder how. Yet even
at its extremity, there is meaning in a life that on the surface may
look meaningless.

A man of eighty sat in my office telling me of his wife to whom he
had been married some fifty years. She had developed Alzheimer's
disease and required total care, which this man was trying to give her
at home. When I asked him why he didn't put her in a convalescent
home, a gentle look came over his face.

"Sometimes I don't know why," he started to explain, "but at night
when she's asleep lying in bed next to me, she's herself again. I hold
her, and look at her; and I have my wife again for just a little while."

A short while later the woman died suddenly of a heart attack.
By the time she died, her husband had become accustomed to
doing without her. During that long transition between earth and
Heaven, however, unknown to her until eternity, she had been a
comfort to her grieving husband. She had helped him get used to

her dying. Even with the worst symptoms of her disease, her life had been meaningful.

* * *

When old age is ravaged by a disease like Alzheimer's, however, counseling can provide support for the caretakers involved. Balance in considering each person's needs is necessary. Every living being deserves dignity; a person who needs total care still deserves privacy, gentleness, and compassion. However, the caretakers also deserve consideration in the sense of encouragement in knowing how far they should be directly involved in caring for their elderly loved ones. Providing a sounding board in order to determine those boundaries, helping caretakers declare those boundaries to other family members, and then helping them cut the recordings of guilt, which often exist regardless of how much they are doing, can be a valuable service.

It is popular in the times in which we live to declare our independence of the elderly or the handicapped. We don't want anything to clutter up our neatly planned lives. Yet in the end such selfishness breeds emptiness and even exacerbates our own fears of who will be there for us when we are in need. Most of us realize that as we treat the aged and the handicapped in our lives, so will our children learn to treat us.

For all they did for us in raising us and influencing us when we were young, the elderly deserve care in their old age. On a higher level still, for those of us who claim to be Christians and as such are obligated to live up to a very high standard of love, it is a biblical principle that we are to help those who are helpless and need our care. In those families where there was abuse or neglect in childhood, there is the greater challenge of Christian love that returns good for evil.

However, caretakers who are driven by guilt to become self-made martyrs help no one. It is wise to take breaks and to know one's limitations in caretaking.

After my mother's death a number of years ago, my Aunt Lydia, who was in the same accident as my mother, was also close to death. For days we did not even tell her of my mother's death. When at last she was stabilized, she was released from the hospital to a convalescent home for two or three weeks of further recovery. It was a chance for those of us who had been responsible for her care to have a brief respite. I remember feeling some guilt over leaving her for what ended up to be a long weekend. But a sense of perspective won out. By leaving town for a much-needed change, we would be better equipped in the long run to take care of her. A vacation was good economy. Of course, my aunt would rather have had us stay, but she understood.

* * *

For many of the aged, however, practical usefulness, the ability to perform a task, is certainly not necessarily obliterated by the passage of time. Old age is not always debilitating. The book *Our Aging Society* reminds us of the increase in life expectancy that has occurred since the beginning of the last century, when the average person lived only forty-seven years. Now, as we are well into the twenty-first century, sixty-five is too soon for most people to retire, much less die.

The authors speak of the third quarter of life, the period between fifty and seventy-five, as a time of active productivity.[3] To those who deal with the elderly, and who are in that middle period of life, the concept of the third quarter should be an encouraging signpost – fifty is no longer over the hill – even if you consider active productivity to be the only form of meaning in this world.

The concept of the third quarter has been more than validated in my experience. I have seen people who are even *beyond* that third-quarter mark and yet are as active as the general population: a psychiatrist in his late seventies who still practices in spite of poor health and whose advice is as clear and sharp as ever; a pastor whose insights into the Scriptures have only deepened with the passage of the years; a violin maker whose hands still reflect skills that have been honed to perfection from years of practice.

Not long ago as I was leaving a dinner party, I stopped to say good-bye to a man I have known most of my life. He is now in his late eighties, although he looks much younger. He was telling me about some artistic projects he wanted to finish, when his wife came over and added, "Phil needs to hire someone to do the yard work so that he can devote more time to his art. There are so many things he wants to do."

Too many things to do and not enough time to do them is not a state that fits our national stereotype of the elderly person who needs help in filling his or her days with relatively useless tasks. Former President Ronald Reagan, who in his late seventies fulfilled his duties with the vigor of a man much younger in years, did not fit the stereotype either. Nor did the ambassador from Sweden, the late Per Anger. When I wrote his biography, which included hours of interviews, I was struck with his keenness of thinking. Yet the stereotype lives on, and even old people and those of us who love them often feed into it.

* * *

Counseling the elderly is seen by some to be fairly nonproductive. "Old people don't change," they explain. In my experience as a family counselor, I have found that many elderly people change a great deal and some young people are already set in their ways. However, if counseling is to become a safety zone of change for the elderly, so that they can truly use these later years in their lives, it is vital that the young as well as the old believe that aging is not a curse but a blessing.

In *The Human Cycle,* Colin Turnbull describes certain African and Indian societies:

> The retirement expected of the aged does indeed also suppose that they retire from active participation in subsistence activities. But this is generally seen to be partly because they are no longer physically fitted to fill that economic role, or because there are others better fitted for that work, but more importantly because there are other things that need to be done and which only the old can do. ... They are relieved of one set of responsibilities so that they can fulfill another, equally vital role.[4]

Especially with the work potential extending into and through the third quarter of life, many people grow elderly more slowly. They can be a part of the main work force of this society for a much longer time. It is important, however, that this "extra" period of productivity be used because it is desired rather than frantically grabbed at as a reprieve against what is seen as the inevitable curse of retirement and old age. The third quarter should not be used to hide from the aging process. When the years catch up and some kind of retirement is necessary, there are tasks to be done for which *only* the elderly are suited. The tasks of old age are unique.

In my family some of us used to joke about my Aunt Lydia being the historian of the family. She was. In her late eighties she could still remember birthdays of those of us who never could remember anyone else's. She could recite long pieces of poetry in a way that reminded those of us who were too caught up in the *doing* of life of the value of refurbishing the spirit. She saved wedding announcements, pictures, newspaper clippings, wills, letters, bills of sale, and numerous other memorabilia from more than a hundred years ago. She could identify a picture of someone like Aunt Sophie in Sweden, whom I had never even heard about. Aunt Lydia not only performed a service by her memory of family history and her practice of collecting documents, but also in so doing cultivated a sense of the continuity of life in younger family members. We learned about the past from her. Most important, we learned about our past from someone who had been an active part of that past. Her task was unique.

* * *

As I was growing up, we lived next door to a German family who became very close to us. When I was in those early formative years, I remember thinking that these neighbor children were so lucky because their grandparents came to live with them. The grandparents babysat their grandchildren in a way that few paid persons ever would. After all, they were their grandchildren. Moreover, while the children were being taken care of physically, they learned about their past.

Our family benefited, too. Sometimes we heard their stories about the "olden times," or we tasted the venison the grandfather smoked periodically in the outside "garden house." Recipes from the grandmother were enjoyed and then handed down, and fortunately for me they were passed across the fence to my mother and ultimately to me.

Some of these recipes have become comfort food, reminding me of good times in the past and again fostering in me that sense of the continuity of life. The old German pancake recipe, for example, brings back childhood memories of spending the night next door, of sleeping in the backyard and then sneaking back in because we were afraid, and of eating our breakfast of pancakes served with homemade syrup and freshly squeezed juice made from tangerines growing in our neighbors' backyard.

These recollections are a whole set of memories that are different from those associated with my mother's Swedish pancakes, which were made thin like crepes and then rolled up with syrup or strawberry jam. My mother's pancakes were a reminder of other special times, sometimes served for company, at times made on rainy or gloomy days, or frequently served as Sunday night supper. Always they were accompanied by an ample supply of bacon. They, too, were comfort food, and both recipes continue to be comfort food in the present for both families, recipes handed down from those who have gone on before.

* * *

Regardless of the meaningfulness of tasks uniquely suited to those who are elderly, there is no reason why, as we age, we should retire from our regular work before we need to or must. We don't have to go from the extreme of avoiding the aging process to the other extreme of prematurely embracing it. Moreover, when we have retired, there is nothing wrong with enjoying life, taking trips abroad, cultivating a hobby, and enjoying the comradeship of other elderly people. To fill up retirement time with shuffleboard and bingo, just because there's nothing else to do, however, is to waste a very valuable period of life. We as a nation and as individuals often waste the vast resources of old age.

An older lady who recently found herself alone and without family was advised by many to go to a senior center for recreation. Later she told me, "I know that places like these meet the needs of many, but not mine. I've decided to work with children who can't read. I have the time, and that's partly what they need." For her, helping children develop a love for the written word has been a fulfilling task, and it has provided a valuable resource for the community.

Teaching children was a rewarding task for *her*; it would not be for others. The unique function of the last years of life should be considered as carefully and prepared for as completely as that of any other time of life. These times are not throwaway years any more than any other period of life.

* * *

Although I do not advocate lengthening the *actual* dying process beyond its time or approve of ridiculous attempts to keep a dead body "alive" long after it was meant to be let go, I do believe in living life to its full length and in valuing life at every stage. I am deeply concerned when the years of old age are looked on as throwaway years, at best to be enjoyed in a limited way with amusements designed to satisfy the superficial whims of a second childhood. Such an attitude is contrary to the biblical concept that age is a reward, a time of honor, and a time of instructing those who are younger.

In his New Testament letter to Titus, Paul commands Titus:

> Teach the older men to be serious and unruffled; they must be sensible, knowing and believing the truth and doing everything with love and patience. Teach the older women to be quiet and respectful…they should be teachers of goodness. These older women must train the younger women.…
>
> (Titus 2:2-4 TLB)

These, too, are part of the works of old age. It is the obligation of the church to teach such a view of old age to its members. In that way, children will take such an attitude for granted as they grow up. Caretakers of the elderly will treat them with respect, with the result that the elderly will take themselves seriously and act with greater dignity. Again, we tend to become what people expect us to become.

Activities for the elderly should not be mere amusements to placate their restlessness or to keep them from bothering anyone. Studies show that social activities can actually help in maintaining the health of the brain. Also, the seriousness of these tasks restores the dignity of age to a society that has at times so drastically lost that sense of dignity that it must go to the Third World for examples of the value of old age, a value based on its proximity to death and its reservoir of knowledge from the past.

In speaking of those who retire and are through with the physically productive period of their lives, Colin Turnbull concludes:

> Those who dream only of all the things they are going to "do" fail to find the state of grace in just being. And the more they try to do, the more they find that they cannot do; the longer and harder they try, the more the recognition of their ultimate failure is impressed upon them. Their golf handicap increases; they win fewer and fewer games of chess; their fingers are less nimble on the keyboard; increasingly they forget to water their prize-winning flowers; their eyesight fails them and makes it difficult and painful to read those unread books. They compete with themselves as well as with others and with life itself to the bitter end....
>
> The more an adult is convinced of his worth at retirement, the harder it is for him to navigate the transition into an old age which we have made into a world of doing nothing. Its patent emptiness and irrelevance to anyone but their

isolated selves often leads to rapid physical or mental deterioration and premature death, or even to suicide. The stereotyped suicide notes that say, "Nobody wants me" and "I am of no use to anyone anymore" are not necessarily penned by individuals in a moment of self-pity; they may well be simple, sober assessments of an agonizing and protracted reality to which, for a socially conscious human being in our individualistic society, only one answer may seem logical.[5]

* * *

If we live long enough, we grow old. The only way to avoid old age is to die young. If we are old long enough, our active productivity will diminish. Our bodies and even our minds may slow down. It is then that we can *be*. To just be can open up more widely unique ways of pleasing God. We can worship God from a different vantage point than ever before. More than ever, we can praise Him for all that He has done, but we can also worship Him for all that He is.

In speaking of the Old Testament offerings in his book on *Numbers*, regarding the burnt offering, CHM explains:

> ...the character of the offering is as plain as possible. It was Christ to Godward. This is the special point in the burnt offering. The sin offering is Christ to usward. In this, it is a question of the hatefulness of sin; in that, it is a question of the preciousness and excellency of Christ....

> But are we not prone to confine our thoughts of Christ to what *He did for us*, to the virtual

exclusion of what *He is to God*? It is this we have
to mourn over and judge, – this we must seek to
have corrected... [6]

Then the question:

Why is there so little in our midst to refresh the
heart of God?

And, once again:

Ought we not to be sufficiently at leisure from
ourselves, when we assemble in His presence,
to be able to present to Him something beside
our own things? He has provided for us. He has
made all right for us. Our sins and our sorrows
have been divinely met. [7]

We often confuse praise with worship. We praise God for what
He has done, but how much do we worship Him for Who He is?
This may well be one of the great privileges of old age in particular
when there is more time and hopefully greater spiritual depth.

* * *

In the area of intercessory prayer, we can also offer up the work
of prayer for others with insight that is forbidden to the very young.
Furthermore, in old age more than at any other time, even if our
memories are faulty, we can provide an actual connection with the
past for those who are younger. It is then that we can be a vital link
in the continuity of life.

My friend the late Joseph Fabry escaped from Austria and
eventually Europe during the time of Hitler's takeover. In his
book, co-written with a lifelong friend, Dr. Fabry describes his
discouragement when, after reaching America, he realized the
dismal prospects for getting his parents out of Europe. In the letters

he received from home, he learned that friends and relatives had gradually disappeared, and my friend realized with increasing clarity that his roots were being ripped away from him. He had experienced a violent disruption in the continuity of life.

In *One and One Make Three*, Dr. Fabry explains:

> As so often happened, one significant incident provided a hint of an answer. I chatted with a woman who helped Horch translate his German authors. She was a seventh-generation American, her ancestor having come two hundred years ago. I said, I wished I had an ancestor like that, and she replied: "Why, *you* are an ancestor." This chance remark shifted my attention from shortcomings in the past to potentials in the future. I lost my family in Europe but could start my own in America! ... a search had begun for a new relatedness.[8]

He had started the beginning of a new thread of the continuity of life, a thread he has now passed on to his children and their children.

We all need that sense of the continuity of our own individual lives on this earth. We need to be part of a past that is bigger than any one person. The elderly provide this for us, sometimes just in our memories of them long after they have left this earth. Not long ago on a St. Patrick's Day I was in my office, listening to a patient, when I heard an old Irish melody playing on the radio in the next room. My Swedish father was very fond of Irish tunes and would often sing or whistle one. The song on the radio had been one of his favorites. For a moment I felt a warm closeness to my father, who died a number of years ago. Happy memories flooded back, and I went on through the day with a sense of security that connected my past with my present and my future. Partly because of my father, my life was part of a whole; it had continuity.

* * *

When I was twelve, my mother and I went back to our old home in Chicago for the summer. It was a time of sight-seeing and visiting relatives. On a hot Sunday afternoon, my mother and I went to Great-aunt Christine's house for a small family reunion. I was the only child present that I remember, and at first I felt a little left out. The house was a lovely old structure, well kept up and impeccably furnished. All the chairs had white lace doilies on their backs and the tables had ruffled doilies under the lamps and vases. Everything was starched, and clean, and perfect. In the middle of it all was Great-aunt Christine, her white hair softly rolled up on top of her head with a perfection that equaled that of the house. Everyone sat drinking coffee from finely decorated china cups, and the conversation flowed around me.

"Would you like a glass of cold grape juice?" It was my Great-aunt Christine's son, Warner Sallman, who had painted the well-beloved head of Christ. He was probably the only famous person there, but to a child he was more impressive for his kindness than for his paintings. I don't remember what else he or anyone else said after that, but I do remember that I suddenly felt part of this group of people. Even though I didn't know most of them, they were my family. Someday I would be grown-up like them and drink coffee or maybe even tea from china cups instead of grape juice from a glass. Someday I would be respected and honored like Great-aunt Christine. I was part of a whole, I was connected; and for the moment at the center of that wholeness was an elderly lady whom I would never really know well personally but whom I would never forget. I didn't learn any family history from her, but on that hot afternoon so long ago, all that was needed was for her just to be.

That was the unique function of her old age and because of that encounter I learned a new positive view of growing old.

* * *

As the race of life slows down for the elderly, others, themselves at varying stages of aging, watch anxiously by the sidelines. For them the aging of those they love is a signpost of what is ahead. They are reminded that they, too, will sometime age and die. They may try to deny the realities of old age by cheering the elderly on to almost lethal doses of activity or they may begin to ignore their elderly friends and relatives, or prematurely put them into so-called retirement homes, where they'll be "with their own kind," as though they were some new breed of human being. They make excuses not to visit. They pretend that the elderly are not there. They deny their existence and then use the fast deterioration of the elderly as further proof of the curse of old age, rather than realizing that the deterioration has been, in part, a result of their own attitude of discouragement.

From the point of view of the inevitable aging process there is on the horizon some encouragement in the area of brain chemistry. While the human brain is made up of 100 billion neurons that number has always been assumed to be fixed at birth. In recent years new advances in brain studies have brought potential hope to the aging process as well as for those who suffer from diseases like Parkinson's, multiple sclerosis, Alzheimer's, and cancer. In a landmark 1998 announcement in the November 1 issue of *Nature America* the results of a study on neurogenesis in the adult hippocampus were revealed: new neurons are produced in the brain, an ability which continues throughout life. The study was conducted by Dr. Fred Gage and his team at the Salk Institute in La Jolla, California, in conjunction with Peter S. Eriksson and his team in Göteberg, Sweden.

A similar announcement by the Salk Institute stated:

> Like bubbles fizzing from fine champagne, it has long been assumed that our supply of brain cells steadily diminishes through our lives, never to be replenished. According to a landmark Salk study, however, new cells are born in human brains, even in mature individuals....
>
> "All of the patients showed evidence of recent cell division," said Salk Professor Fred H. Gage, senior author on the study.[9]

In a July 1, 2008, press release the Salk Institute revealed even greater progress:

> In recent years, stem cell researchers have become very adept at manipulating the fate of adult stem cells cultured in the lab. Now, researchers at the Salk Institute for Biological Studies achieved the same feat with adult neural stem cells still in place in the brain....
>
> The discovery... not only attests to the versatility of neural stem cells but also opens up new directions for the treatment of neurological diseases, such as multiple sclerosis, stroke and epilepsy...

According to Sebastian Jessberger, M.D., assistant professor at the Institute of Cell Biology at the Swiss Federal Institute of Technology in Zurich, "It was quite surprising that stem cells in the adult brain maintain their fate plasticity and that a single gene was enough to reprogram these cells...We can now potentially tailor the fate of stem cells to treat certain conditions such as multiple sclerosis.'"[10]

There is, therefore, more hope for the course of the aging process and its accompanying disorders than previously thought. According to Dr. John Ratey, "Aging is unavoidable; severe memory loss is not."[11]

In an interview with Dr. Gage on *Science Watch*, November/December 2005, Dr. Gage talked about research to repair the Central Nervous System (CNS) after an injury. Once again, the plasticity of the brain as well as neurogenesis may have potential in the treatment of various disorders and in the loss of cells in the aging process. Explained Dr. Gage:

> Everything I have done so far in the CNS leads me to believe that the nervous system tries to repair itself after an injury. It does this at one level or another, and usually it accomplishes some moderate level of recovery. I'm less interested now in engineering from the outside and transplanting cells, but rather in activating and amplifying the existing cell-repair process that's already there in the CNS. I think this harks back to the original reasons I was interested in the brain. It has this capacity for self-repair... [12]

* * *

Besides waiting for ongoing research, and adding good nutrition, meaningful social involvement, proper medications, and talk therapy, when needed, perhaps the most important practical antidote for aging is to be found in exercise. According to most research a chemical called brain-derived neutrotrophic factor or BDNF is the fuel which enables the growth of neurons. It is built up in the body by exercise. Aerobic exercises have been shown to be effective.

"Dopamine, serotonin, norepinephrine – all of these are elevated after a bout of exercise," says Ratey. "So having a workout will help with focus, calming down, impulsivity – it's like taking a little bit of Prozac and a little bit of Ritalin."[13]

Some have noted that not only exercise but exercise which requires cognitive thought and change, like tennis, dance, or volleyball, are even more helpful in boosting brain cells. But the emphasis on exercise is no longer aiming only at increased blood flow to the brain. It is far bigger and more helpful than that.

Variations on these themes would obviously need to be worked out for people who are not able to run around a tennis court. The first steps in such help have already begun. In a July 31, 2008, press release the Salk Institute stated the following:

> Trying to reap the health benefits of exercise? Forget treadmills and spin classes, researchers at the Salk Institute for Biological Studies may have found a way around the sweat and pain. They identified two signaling pathways that are activated in response to exercise and converge to dramatically increase endurance.
>
> The team of scientists, led by Howard Hughes Medical Investigator Ronald M. Evans, Ph.D., a professor in the Salk Institute's Gene Expression Laboratory, report in the July 31 advance online edition of the journal *Cell* that simultaneously triggering both pathways with oral drugs turned laboratory mice into long-distance runners and conferred many of exercise's other benefits.
>
> In addition to their allure for endurance athletes, drugs that mimic the effect of exercise

have therapeutic potential in treating certain muscle diseases, such as wasting and frailty, as well as obesity and a slew of associated metabolic disorders where exercise is known to be beneficial.[14]

Truly "exercise in a pill."

* * *

If watching the elderly grow older is a signpost to the young of what is ahead, the actual death of a parent is a blinking red light of one's own mortality. The day before my mother's funeral was a very trying day for me. I had expected to feel down, but I had not expected to feel a sort of nagging anxiety as though something I could not completely identify was wrong. I read my Bible; I took a hot bubble bath; I talked to some friends; I went out to dinner. I did all the things I usually do to relax, and none of them helped.

Then I picked up a copy of Madeleine L'Engle's *The Summer of the Great Grandmother*. Toward the end of the book the author makes the comment, "I will never again be anyone's child." In that one statement I recognized my own feelings. That was the anxiety. In my mother's death I had passed another signpost. She was the second parent to die. The last. I was now truly adult. I was now the authority rather than the one who still, once in a while, looked to my mother's authority. I had been an adult for a long time. But now there was no turning back. Moreover, not only was I now completely adult, but also I had moved up a notch in that inevitable journey toward my own death.

With the recognition of my own feelings in that simple line, "I will never again be anyone's child," a great peace settled upon me. I knew what was wrong, and it was not "wrong" at all. I had seen the signpost: "You are now *the* adult; you will never again be anyone's child." The signpost had frightened me at first. Then, when I understood what the signpost was truly saying, I felt that I had been promoted to a new position of responsibility and challenge. I felt that God was now calling me to provide to those around me the support and help that I had received from my mother and from others like her. The next day I went to my mother's funeral with grief but also with hope for the future.

* * *

Seventeenth-century poet John Donne's idea that no man is an island and that every man's death diminishes each of us is true in connection with our view of the elderly in a different sense, perhaps, than that meant by Donne. Their death diminishes us because we fear that we are next in line. We make feeble attempts to ignore the elderly, as if by denying their existence we can reaffirm the myth that we ourselves will never age, or at least not in the near future!

At the same time we are busy denying the aging process in others, in our own lives we gloomily prepare for our own aging with over-the-hill jokes about that milestone birthday *fifty*. We are filled with regret rather than the reward of the years. Anti-aging creams and cosmetic surgery postpone the ravages of time for yet a while. All this because, above all, we ourselves fear the specter of age and ultimately death.

The Judeo-Christian tradition has always included a belief in the hereafter. Yet to many of us old age still marks the End and thus becomes something to avoid.

In contrast, other cultures that believe in an afterlife view the proximity of the aged to death or eternity as something very positive. They are revered because they become a link to the spirit world. Anthropologist Colin Turnbull says:

> Certainly in other cultures, particularly those
> with a firm belief in an after or other life, the

> old are accorded a position of often enormous respect and honor....They are ignored, in our society, for the very thing that makes them so immensely powerful in other societies: their proximity to death. That is, perhaps, what we need most to explore, this association in other cultures of the old with that vast source of power, Spirit power, that lies beyond death. It provides a whole new perspective on old age.[15]

Lest this sound too mystical to us, let us remember that we Christians, too, have our own perspective on Spirit power that can be of great help and comfort to us. In spite of the fact that our culture has abused the reality of and blurred the meaning of a term like *Spirit power* by our society's focus on demonic or even so-called neutral supernatural forces, Heaven and God Almighty still exist. We still deal with a supernatural God with supernatural powers that far outdo anything Satan can attempt to imitate. Indeed, such imitation on the part of Satan is to be expected, for if there is no reality, there is no counterfeit.

Long before Turnbull used the term, and long before the concept became perverted into occult connotations, men and women of God have evidenced a sense of Spirit power in their treatment of old age and death. Within us is an innate need for a God Connection. Old Testament saints did not avoid deathbed scenes: a deathbed was often a place where the dying person – this person who was now so close to Heaven – spoke wise words to those who remained.

When King David was about to die, he spoke to his son Solomon:

> I am going where every man on earth must some day go. I am counting on you to be a strong and worthy successor. Obey the laws of God and follow all his ways; keep each of his

commands written in the law of Moses so that you will prosper in everything you do, wherever you turn. If you do this, then the Lord will fulfill the promise he gave me, that if my children and their descendants watch their step and are faithful to God, one of them shall always be the king of Israel – my dynasty will never end. (1 Kings 2:2-4 LL)

Consistent with the deathbed exhortation of King David, the Old Testament deathbed was often the scene of the conferring of a blessing. In Genesis 27:4, Isaac is old and is anticipating his death when he asks Esau to "make me savoury meat ... that I may eat; that my soul may bless thee before I die." In their commentary Jamieson, Fausset, and Brown note:

The deathbed benediction of the patriarchs was not simply the last farewell blessing of a father to his children, though that, pronounced with all the fulness and energy of concentrated feeling, carries in every word an impressive significance which penetrates the inmost parts of the filial heart, and is often felt there long after the tongue that uttered it is silent in the grave. The dying benediction of the patriarchs had a mysterious import; it was a supernatural act ... It was, in fact, a testamentary conveyance of the promise, bequeathed with great solemnity in a formal address, called a *blessing*; which, consisting partly of prayers and partly of predictions, was an authoritative appropriation of the covenant promises to the person who inherited the right of primogeniture.[16]

* * *

This God connection is more clearly understandable to the Christian in the familiar yet often ignored words of Hebrews 12:1: "Wherefore seeing we also are compassed about with so great a cloud of witnesses, let us lay aside every weight, and the sin which doth so easily beset us, and let us run with patience the race that is set before us." Those who have gone before are still linked with us. They cheer us on. Those who are closer by age to death than we are, but who are still with us, are becoming a link with us to eternity.

I experienced something of the truth of Hebrews 12:1 after my mother's death, when I wrote in my personal journal:

> I am alone. I will never again be anyone's child. But I can go on and live in my friendships and do and become those things which were meant for my life – my writing, my therapy – and above all honor God. In these ways I will deserve my parents' trust in me. I love them both and will always miss them. But I must go on, for "I have miles to go before I sleep."

Most of my relatives were in Heaven when I wrote those words, but I still felt the comfort of my family's approval; I was motivated by my belief that they were now, perhaps more than ever before, cheering me on. On earth they saw in part, but now they have seen our Lord face-to-face, and they see the whole.

In Old Testament history, while Israel was still in the wilderness after leaving Egypt, God told Moses to send spies into Canaan to "search the land" (Num. 13:2). They were to bring back a report on the unknown to those who were still safely behind its borders. Some told of giants in the land; others spoke of a land that flowed with milk and honey.

Part of the special Spirit power of those who grow old and approach Heaven is that they tell us what they see as they approach the Land. They make a report. To some there are giants in the transition between life and death. There can be a fear of the process of dying, even when people know Christ and are therefore sure of their eternal destiny after death. Dying is not always just falling asleep. Sometimes it involves pain and struggle. For until we are actually with God, we still cope with the frailty of this human body of ours. But for the Christian who looks beyond the human discomfort, the Land itself "floweth with milk and honey" (Num. 13:27).

> But what will be the blessedness when Jesus does come? Well, a part of that blessedness will be *in future service*. You must not think that, when you have done working here, you Sunday-school teachers, and those of us who preach and teach, that the Master will say, "I have discharged you from my service. Go and sit on a heavenly mount, and sing yourselves away for ever and ever." Not a bit of it. I am but learning how to preach now; I shall be able to preach by-and-by. You are only learning to teach now; you will be able to teach by-and-by. Yes, to angels, and principalities, and powers, you shall make known the manifold wisdom of God. I sometimes aspire to the thought of a congregation of angels and archangels, who shall sit and wonder, as I tell what God has done for me; and I shall be to them an everlasting monument of the grace of God to an unworthy wretch, upon whom he looked with infinite compassion, and saved with a wonderful salvation.

All those stars, those worlds of light, who knows how many of them are inhabited? I believe there are regions beyond our imagination to which every child of God shall become an everlasting illumination, a living example of the love of God in Christ Jesus. The people in those far distant lands could not see Calvary as this world has seen it; but they shall hear of it from the redeemed. Remember how the Lord will say, "Well done, thou good and faithful servant: thou hast been faithful over a few things, I will make thee ruler over many things." He is to keep on doing something, you see. Instead of having some little bit of a village to govern, he is to be made ruler over some great province. So it is in this passage. Read the forty-fourth verse: "Of a truth I say unto you, that he will make him ruler over all that he hath." That is, the man who has been a faithful and wise steward of God here, will be called of God to more eminent service hereafter. If he serve his Master well, when his Master comes, he will promote him to still higher service.

Do you not know how it used to be in the Spartan army? Here is a man who has fought well, and been a splendid soldier. He is covered with wounds on his breast. The next time that there is a war, they say, "Poor fellow, we will reward him! He shall lead the way in the first battle. He fought so well before, when he met one hundred with a little troop behind him; now he shall meet ten thousand with a larger troop."

"Oh!" say you, "that is giving him more work." That is God's way of rewarding his people, and a blessed thing it is for the industrious servant. His rest is in serving God with all his might. This shall be our heaven, not to go there to roost, but to be always on the wing; for ever flying, and for ever resting at the same time. "They do his commandments, hearkening unto the voice of his word." "His servants shall serve him: and they shall see his face."[17]

A number of years ago as my father lay on a hospital bed close to death, he was asked how things were with him. He replied succinctly, "It is the grace of God which has brought me thus far, and it is that grace of God which will bring me through." He gave a good report of that Land to which he was going.

I remembered years before when as a child I used to hear him stand up in the mid-week prayer meeting and recite the Twenty-third Psalm: "...though I walk through the valley of the shadow of death, I will fear no evil: for thou art with me..." Now, close to the time of his departure to be with his Lord, the report was still good. His words encouraged me more than anything else at that time. It became his gift to me as he died. It was his truest legacy to his children. The Land to which he was going was okay; we didn't need to fear aging and death.

Furthermore, even in his dying my father showed that there was meaning both to himself and to those around him. Although the process of dying is not something that most of us look forward to, for those who have placed their faith in Christ physical death itself means to be in the presence of our Lord. Unless we choose to end our lives ourselves, that precise moment in our history when we are ushered into His presence has been determined by God from before the foundation of the earth. The timing of each of our deaths is no mistake. Death is not limited to the aged. But whatever our life span, we do not need to fear that we will not finish the course that God has set for us. Our living and our dying are in His time.

* * *

To those who are not old but fear what will happen to them when they are old, Charles Spurgeon has some very comforting words:

> Now, you middle-aged men, you are plunged into the midst of business, and are sometimes supposing what will become of you in your old age….You say, "Suppose I should live to be as old as So-and-so, and be a burden upon the people, I should not like that." Don't get meddling with God's business; leave his decrees to him. There is many a person who thought he would die in a workhouse that has died in a mansion; and many a woman that has thought she would die in the streets, has died in her bed, happy and comfortable.… Middle-aged man! listen to what David says again, "I have been young, and now am old; yet I have not seen the righteous forsaken, nor his seed begging bread." Go on, then…leave thy declining years to him, and give thy present years to him.[18]

In a society that attempts to deny death, even when we are in its very presence, by trying to make the dead look "natural" in their coffins, it is perhaps to be expected that we should deny death before it occurs by hiding the elderly and pretending that we ourselves are not so close to death after all. Yet, more often than not, in confronting such fears rather than denying them we see them in their true perspective.

To provide a place for such confrontation has traditionally been the province of the church. Yet increasingly I have people come into the safety zone of my counseling office in order to sort out and discuss without fear of censure their views, doubts, and fears regarding death and what comes after death.

In the 1951 movie version of Stephen Crane's *Red Badge of Courage*, a young man fighting in the Civil War fears death in battle and fears fear itself. After the agony of experiencing the cowardice of running from battle and the exhilaration of great courage as he carries the flag into the greatest heat of battle, he goes home in triumph over his fear. At the end the narrator says, "As he trudged from the place of blood and wrath his soul changed. He had been to touch the Great Death and found that, after all, it was but the Great Death."

In the same way we, too, deal with our own mortality as we deal with the aged. In childhood and youth we feel immortal. The young are reckless because they do not yet appreciate the frailty of life. As we view those around us growing old, and even the young sometimes dying, we begin to view our own mortality. Our relationship with the aged can provide a graceful transition between youth and age for us which, if we miss it, just makes our own aging that much more difficult. Ultimately, as we view others' transition into old age, we find that, as well as being mortal on this earth, we are truly immortal souls.

"Now no chastening for the present seemeth to be joyous, But grievous: nevertheless afterward it yieldeth the peaceable fruit of righteousness unto them which are exercised thereby."

Hebrews 12:11

Written June 26, 2008

These things shall pass,
And so in one grand vista
of brightness,
All clouds fall from the sky;
for though the clouds may
not pass away now,
Then in heaven shall they
fly away.

These things shall pass,
and some grand morn,
"God shall wipe all tears
from" your eyes.
So you can see the
"nevertheless afterward"
of His redeeming grace,
And you shall know the
beauty of his love.

– Elizabeth S. Wilcox

TEN

MAKING BAD TIMES GOOD

*F*or months Neil had been sleeping with various women he met on business trips. His wife, Margarita, had never found out about any of the affairs, but she had noticed an emotional wall rising between them. Then suddenly one Monday afternoon Neil called home to tell Margarita that he was leaving her for good. "You're fat and ugly!" he exclaimed with cruelty. "I want someone younger."

The truth was that Margarita had remained slim and attractive but Neil had put on thirty pounds during the preceding year. That fact, added to his celebration of his fortieth birthday, a milestone he commemorated by spending the day getting drunk, was probably the real motivator in spurring Neil to find out how attractive he could still be to women.

Margarita was left with four children: two teenage sons and two children of grammar-school age. Neil's support checks were sporadic. Because Margarita had never worked outside her home, she was panicky at first. Then someone advised her, "Just think about what you do best and do it."

Margarita had developed into a wonderful cook over the past two decades. A friend had been having trouble making a success of a small snack bar, even though it was well located near some construction sites. The friend made a gentleman's agreement with Margarita that if she could make the snack bar at least break even, he would give her a partnership in the business and share the proceeds with her.

Full of excitement, Margarita went to work. She decided that the snack bar drew little interest because the food was not only routine and dull but also poorly prepared. An expert in soups, Margarita started making her own homemade specialties, a different soup every day. She served the soup with freshly baked corn bread. Her cooking was a success. People not only flocked there for lunch, but also called ahead to reserve bowls of soup. Within six months the snack bar was a real money-maker.

Then one morning the owner came in to visit. "I appreciate all you've done," he commented, after obtaining copies of her recipes. "This is great soup." Then he explained that he was going to let his son take over the business; he wouldn't need her anymore. There was no contract. After all, they had been friends, and she had trusted him.

As Margarita told me her story two years later, it made *me* angry, even if she did seem to be handling it. "That's okay," she said reassuringly. "I got something from it. I learned that everyone liked my homemade soup and corn bread. I was okay, after all."

As a counselor I have discovered that a determining factor in how much difficulty we have with handling hard times is whether we view our cup as half empty or half full. In a sense Margarita had lost it all: her husband, her source of income, and even her faith in a friend. However, she saw that her cup was half full. She had proven to herself that Neil's problems were his own. She was okay. With her confidence restored, she has been paid in currency more precious than gold.

* * *

During recent years, it seems to me, we have had an inordinate number of natural disasters across this country. Floods, hurricanes, earthquakes, tornados, and fires have filled the nightly news reports. Through the rather bizarre way reporters have of interviewing people just as disaster has devastated their lives, we sometimes gain remarkable insight into people's immediate reactions to personal loss and bad times.

After a disaster, two general groups of people seem to emerge. One says, understandably, "Everything is gone. I don't know what to do. We've lost everything we've worked for." Another says, pointing to the ashes on the ground, "That's what's left, and the insurance will only cover a small amount of the losses. Photographs and personal belongings can't be replaced. But we're so lucky. No one died. We still have each other."

Many in the first group eventually move over to the second, once the initial shock is past, and a few from the second group may fall back into the first. But how well anyone who experiences bad times can make them into good times will hinge on whether the person focuses on the cup as half full or half empty.

* * *

A while back, after working all evening on paying my bills, I was surprised to find that I was able to pay more bills at one time than I had first anticipated. I went to bed happy over that fact. I still had bills to be paid, but those obligations would be met and my focus was on what I had been able to pay already. My cup was half full.

The next morning I woke up with a jolt. My focus had changed: I still had unpaid bills. All the relief of the previous evening was gone. The night before I had said to myself, "My bills are in pretty good shape." Now, the next morning, I was asking, "What if I can't pay my bills on time?" My cup had become half empty.

After an operation for cancer, someone once said to me, "I'm lucky. Most people live from day to day in a sort of unconscious manner. They assume their days are unlimited. Then suddenly life is over, and they've never really done what they wanted with those days. I've had a red blinking light go off. I *know* my days are limited. I will use those days better now than I would have if I had never had cancer."

When this person related these feelings to her physician, he just shook his head and said, "You have an amazing attitude." In reality, it was a sound attitude. It was looking at a cup as half full rather than half empty. It reminded me of a story I once read of two men in a prison who looked out their prison window. One saw mud, and one saw blue sky.

In the little gray book into which I used to copy quotations from the blackboard during my high school senior English class, one quotation, written by an unknown source, adds an apt insight to the half-empty, half-full image:

> The optimist fell ten stories.
> At each window bar
> He shouted to his friends:
> "All right so far."

Trite? Perhaps. Homey? Definitely. Nevertheless, in these whimsical lines there is truth that has existed throughout human history. Life is deadly serious. Yet, in spite of that seriousness – and perhaps because of it – we dare not embark upon the challenge of living without a sense of humor and the ability to see through the rain to the rainbow.

* * *

Hard times are indeed far from trite. As the late Ruth Bell Graham said in one of my interviews with her: "It's so easy to be superficial or to speak too quickly." Ruth went on, "There are some things that come crushing down on lives that are far too heavy to lift." For those things there is the biblical injunction to commit our way unto the Lord. The Hebrew word for *commit*, she explained, means "to roll." "We can roll something that is so great a weight that we cannot possibly lift it.... It takes years of learning that He never lets us down.... It doesn't mean that He doesn't disappoint us.... He doesn't always give in to us. ... He doesn't always answer our prayers the way we want Him to. But so much the better in the long run."

During the major times of crisis in our lives, the pain may be excruciating at first. An admonition to make lemons into lemonade will only be an insult. Lemonade may come much later, after the raw wounds have healed. Ruth Graham's image for those times that are particularly difficult is that of an *abscess*, which according to the dictionary is "a localized collection of pus surrounded by inflamed tissue." Said Ruth, "You have to let time for an abscess to come to head before you can lance it. ... When you once lance it and the pus is drained off, then the healing can begin. It's a slow process, but it's an important process."

Sometimes the counseling office is the place where abscesses are lanced, and the bitterness, fear, and anger are vented in safety. It is important that enough time is given for this initial process; however, focus must be turned as soon as possible to going on. The cup must once again be viewed as half full. The time must come, too, for making lemonade. For although we cannot always choose the circumstances of our lives, we can choose our attitude toward those circumstances.

Not long ago *Time* magazine carried an article by Richard Behar entitled "Warlocks, Witches and Swastikas." It told of vandalism by four young people against a prominent rabbi, as well as against other Jews. Some wanted the boys exposed by having their names printed in the newspaper; others wanted revenge. In contrast, the rabbi wanted to be part of the healing.

A year prior to the incident, the rabbi had lost his son. A few months after the attack, the rabbi had heart surgery. Yet after the court hearing, he started teaching twenty-five hours of Jewish culture to four boys who had assaulted his home but whom he now invited into his temple. The rabbi had chosen his attitude toward his given set of circumstances. He had focused on healing four boys who had harmed him, rather than focusing on his pain.

* * *

Mark was only five when his mother died and his father abandoned him in a car parked in a vacant lot. The police found him, and he was placed in a foster home with a kindly older couple. For the next year, Mark lived with nightmares of being abandoned. At school the older children teased him about belonging to the state. He became spiteful and vengeful, which only got him into trouble with his teacher. Regular visits from his social worker and occasional interviews by couples who "wanted to take him out and be his 'special friends'" were constant reminders that his placement was temporary and that adoption by some stranger was imminent.

More devastating than anything else, in his mind's eye he kept seeing his father walking away from him in the parking lot, while Mark screamed, "Daddy, Daddy, don't leave me here alone." His father had kept walking until he had disappeared around the corner.

Then one Sunday morning Mark went to Sunday school and learned about Christ. He learned also that Heaven was a place where we would see those we had loved on earth. In his prayers that night, Mark prayed:

> Dear God,
> Please come and live in my life. And please
> make my Daddy love you too. Then we can at
> least live together in heaven.

From that time on, Mark was a much happier little boy. Nothing in his outward circumstances had really changed: his father was still missing, couples still made him their "special friend," and the children at school still teased him. However, Mark had found a heavenly Father who cared about him and who wouldn't abandon him in a parking lot. He had hope, too, of seeing his earthly father again, at least in Heaven. Even at his early age, Mark had changed from seeing a half-empty cup to one that was half full. He had turned his bad times into good.

* * *

Choosing our attitude toward a given set of circumstances is easier, and sometimes only possible, if we look away from the circumstances that surround us to focus on God. Missionary Amy Carmichael was fond of saying, "All that troubles is only for a moment. Nothing is important but that which is eternal."[1] This concept has often held me from resentment and despair as I have realized that God never wastes suffering. Everything that happens to us is allowed or sent by God and has eternal purpose, regardless of whether we understand it all now.

As I was falling asleep the other night, my mind drifted to the theme of making bad times good. It occurred to me that God always carefully measures out our suffering. In contrast, His blessings are poured out upon us freely and without measure. Furthermore, how much we turn unavoidable suffering into blessing by choosing our attitude toward that suffering will be a determining factor in the state of our mental health.

In a striking illustration of how much God may be doing in our lives that we can't understand or see, Charles Spurgeon once preached about a woman who went to a place where they were manufacturing a carpet. As she looked at the carpet which was being made, she said, "There is no beauty there."

The owner objected, "It is one of the most beautiful carpets you ever saw."

Still committed to the idea that the carpet was ugly, the woman criticized, "Why here is a piece hanging out, and it is all in disorder."

"Do you know why, ma'am?" the man said once again, in disagreement. Then, in answer to his own question, he said, "You look at the wrong side."[2]

A friend of mine called recently with a tone of excitement in his voice. "Do you remember the illustration about the carpet, and seeing the wrong side?" he asked. "Well, I just came back from a trip. I went to a factory where they make lovely wall hangings and carpets. It really is just like we heard. Underneath, as you stand on the floor and look up at the loom, the carpet looks terrible. There is no design, and all kinds of different colored loose ends hang down. But then, when someone takes the loom down and shows you the right side, the pattern is beautiful."

Sometimes on this earth we see only the underneath side of what God is making out of our lives. We see the frayed ends and what looks like a meaningless pattern of events. God sees it all from a divine perspective. He sees the beautiful, finished product of our lives. At times He gives us a glimpse of what we are becoming, and we are encouraged. Then, when we focus on the eternal purposes of our lives, our cup once again becomes half full, not half empty.

The safety zone of counseling is a place where people can discover how to make bad times good. For the Christian it can also be a place of discovering the talents God has given us and more about the tapestry God is weaving into our lives.

* * *

A colleague of mine once said, "Life is a little like the ocean. The tide always goes out and it always comes in. When the tide is out, it looks as though it will always stay out. When it is in, it looks as though it will never go back out. But the tide always comes in; and it always goes out. It does not remain constant."

Bad and good times both are the lot of all men and women. This is life. Unlike the tide, however, we each have a choice: we can focus on the retreating tide, which seems to be taking all of our dreams out with it, or we can focus on the fact that the tide truly does come back in with all its fullness. Life changes, for good and for bad, but what we do with what life offers us can make all the difference between making it and not making it in this world. Unlike the inanimate piece of tapestry my friend watched being woven, we humans have a choice in cooperating with what God is making of our lives.

Not long ago a college professor who had been seeing me about work-related issues as well as some self-esteem problems came for his last appointment. When Bill first started his counseling sessions, he was intimidated by what he viewed as his colleagues' superior backgrounds in teaching. Furthermore, his students frightened him, and so his relationship with them was stilted and formal. Like so many people with low self-esteem, Bill focused on himself and on what people thought of him.

As he gained self-esteem and developed skills in declaring and in time management, Bill became an effective teacher. He learned to say "No" to unreasonable demands, and he planned his work so that he had time for more social activities. Understandably, his stress level was greatly reduced.

At his final meeting with me, Bill slumped down into the familiar leather chair, put his feet up on the footstool, and said with a grin, "With all the changes in curriculum this year, I wouldn't have begun to make it a year ago. Now the newness just seems like an enjoyable challenge." What would once have been a nightmare of defeat had become a platform for growth; what other teachers were viewing as a bad year for teaching had become a good year for Bill.

* * *

Recycling is a popular concept in our world in this twenty-first century. Paper products and tin cans that have served their purpose are now made usable again in this time of too much throwaway waste, too little space, and seemingly too many people. Recycling is becoming a necessity for survival.

In the emotional and spiritual realm, recycling is also a necessity for survival. In the safety zone of counseling, people learn to take lives with shattered dreams and rebuild them into something very new and wonderful. Instead of being destroyed by the past, they build in the present; instead of living with regrets over the past, they live in hopes of the future. From the viewpoint of the psychotherapeutic process, talk therapy is in essence what psychotherapist Dr. Susan Vaughan has called it, "talking to neurons." Furthermore she adds that that makes an effective psychotherapist a "microsurgeon of the mind."[3]

In the movie *Shadowlands*, which portrays the latter part of the life of C. S. Lewis, a colleague says to Lewis, "I don't have your faith in divine recycling." For the Christian the recycling process is more than a humanistic attempt to make people better. The Christian God is the Great Recycler, and sometimes He uses the counselor and the place of counseling as tools in His divine recycling.

In speaking of the physical body, Lewis once wrote in a letter:

> Like old automobiles, aren't they? where all sorts of apparently different things keep going wrong, but what they add up to is the plain fact that the machine is wearing out. Well, it was not meant to last forever. Still, I have a kindly feeling for the old rattle-trap. Through it God showed me that whole side of His beauty which is embodied in colour, sound, smell and size.[4]

The same ideas could be expressed regarding the human mind. Who could be better at recycling either the mind or the body, the emotions or the spirit, than the One who designed them and created them to start with?

* * *

Ultimately, therefore, when we speak of counseling and change, we must concur with the well-known psychotherapist Rollo May, who says:

> Finally, after all our discussion, we come to the realization that there is a great area in the transformation of personality which we do not understand, and which we can attribute only to the mysterious creativity of life. ... As the motto has it, "The physician furnishes the conditions – God works the cure." Like the doctor, we may bind up the wound, but there are all the forces of life welling up in their incalculable spontaneity in the growing together of skin and nerve tissues and the reflowing of blood to perform the healing. Before the creative forces of life, the true counselor stands humbly. And his humility is not of the false sort, for the deeper his understanding of personality the more clearly he realizes how minute his efforts in comparison to the greatness of the whole. He says with the psalmist, "Lord, that is too wonderful for me." I am myself frank to say that when the limits of my own understanding are reached. I understand the miracle of transformation of personality in

terms of the age-old but ever new concept, the
grace of God.[5]

After my mother's death there followed a three-year process of working through things, papers, business details, and family problems. Everyone in my family had been dying, seemingly at once, and so I was faced with details involving the deaths of several people, all of whom were very dear to me. Memories were constant, as was my fatigue. Although there were some wonderful times of respite, encouragement, and even happiness, for much of the time my cup had seemed half empty.

On a Friday afternoon shortly before Thanksgiving, after I finished some details that marked, symbolically, the end of the deaths and the beginning of normal life, a friend and I drove up a street toward my apartment. It was a rainy day, the kind where it always looks as if the rain is going to stop but it doesn't. Normally I love rain, but on this particular day the slow drizzle matched my mood: nothing extreme, just flat.

Then I looked up into the rain-filled sky and saw a rainbow. The tightness I had felt inside relaxed. Through blinding tears I watched those soft colors of hope until they finally disappeared into the sky once again, and then I was left with a deep sense of worship and gratitude toward God. My cup had seemed so empty, and now it suddenly seemed so full once again. Culminating in that brief moment, my life had been divinely recycled. Bad times had once again become good.

NOTES

Chapter One: A Safety Zone of Discovery

1   Paul Tournier et al., *A Place for You* (New York: Harper & Row, 1968), 79.

2   Rollo May, *The Art of Counseling* (Nashville: Abingdon, 1967), 119.

3   Tournier *Place* 22.

4   Anton Gill, *The Journey Back from Hell* (New York: William Morrow, 1988), 328.

5   Martin Niemöller, *Dachau Sermons,* trans. Robert H. Pfeiffer (New York and London: Harper & Brothers, 1946), 78-79.

6   Miep Gies with Alison Leslie Gold, *Anne Frank Remembered* (New York: Simon & Schuster, 1987), 139.

7   C. S. Lewis et al., *The Inklings* (Boston: Houghton Mifflin Company, 1979), 45.

8   Sigmund Freud, quoted in M. D. Sackler et al., "Recent Advances in Psychobiology and Their Impact on General Practice," *Inter. Record of Med.* 170 (1957): 1551.

9   Henry Hyde, *For Every Idle Silence* (Ann Arbor: Servant Books, 1985), 108.

Chapter Two: Between the Extremes

1   "American Association of Christian Counselors: Biblical Charlatans," *PsychoHeresy Awareness Letter* vol. 16, no. 2 (March-April 2008), http://www.pamweb.org/aacc_charlatans_16-2.html.

2   J.E. Adams', *The Use of the Scriptures in Counseling* (Philadelphia: Presbyterian and Reformed, 1975), 19-20.

3   J.E. Adams', *The Christian Counselor's Manual* (Grand Rapids: Baker, 1973), 378.

4   C.H. Spurgeon, *The New Park Street Pulpit*, vol. 4, 460-61.

5   Jay E. Adams', *Competent to Counsel* (Phillipsburg, NJ: Presbyterian and Reformed, 1970), 15.

6   Sigmund Freud, *An Outline of Psychoanalysis*, (New York: W. W. Norton, 1949).

7   Sigmund Freud, quoted in M. D. Sackler et al., "Recent Advances in Psychobiology and Their Impact on General Practice," *Inter. Record of Med.* 170 (1957): 1551.

8   Barry Taylor et al., *An Emergent Manifesto of Hope*, edited by Doug Pagitt and Tony Jones (Grand Rapids: Baker Books, 2007), 166.

9   E. May Grimes, "Speak, Lord, in the Stillness," *Hymns: The hymnal of Inter-Varsity Christian Fellowship*, compiled and edited by Paul Beckwith (Chicago: Inter-Varsity Press, 1959), 98.

10   Thomas Keating, *Open Mind, Open Heart: The Contemplative Dimension of the Gospel* (New York: Continuum, 1997), 140-41.

11.   M. Basil Pennington, Thomas Keating, Thomas E. Clarke, *Finding Grace at the Center* (Petersham, MA: St. Bede's Pub., 1978), 5-6.

12   Andy Crouch, "The Emergent Mystique," *Christianity Today* (November 2004), http://www.christianitytoday.com/ct/2004/november/12.36.html.

13   Tony Jones et al., *An Emergent Manifesto of Hope*, edited by Doug Pagitt and Tony Jones (Grand Rapids: Baker Books, 2007), 129.

14   Taylor *Emergent* 165-66.

15 Samir Selmanovic et al., *An Emergent Manifesto of Hope,* edited by Doug Pagitt and Tony Jones (Grand Rapids: Baker Books, 2007), 194.

16 H. C. G. Moule, *The Second Epistle to Timothy: Short Devotional Studies on the Dying Letter of St. Paul* (Grand Rapids: Baker Book House, 1952), 91-92.

17 Handley C. G. Moule, D.D., *Colossian and Philemon Studies: Lessons in Faith and Holiness* (London: Pickering & Inglis Ltd.), 176-78.

18 Pasquier Quesnel as quoted in Moule *Colossian* 177.

19 Moule *Colossian* 179.

20 Janet I. Tu, "Pastor Mark Packs 'em In," *The Seattle Times: Pacific Northwest Magazine* (November 30, 2003), http://seattletimes.nwsource.com/pacificnw/2003/1130/cover.html.

21 Mark Driscoll et al., *The Supremacy of Christ in a Postmodern World,* edited by John Piper and Justin Taylor (Wheaton: Crossway Books, 2007), 133-134.

22 Larry Crabb, *The Papa Prayer: The Prayer You've Never Prayed* (Nashville: Thomas Nelson, 2006), 9.

23 Crabb *Papa* 22.

24 Chris Armstrong and Steven Gertz, "Christian History Corner: Got Your 'Spiritual Director' Yet?: The roots of a resurgent practice, plus 14 books for further study." *Christianity Today* (Week of April 28, 2003), http://www.christianitytoday.com/ct/2003/117/51.0.html.

25 Larry Crabb interviewed by Ed Rowell, *Leadership Journal* (Fall 2001), http://www.christianitytoday.com/le/2001/004/39.119.html.

26 Agnieszka Tennant, "A Shrink Gets Stretched: Why psychologist Larry Crabb believes spiritual direction should replace therapy." *Christianity Today* (May 2003) http://www.christianitytoday.com/ct/2003/005/7.52.html.

27   Charles H. Spurgeon, "Discouragement," *His* (February 1962), 8.

28   Spurgeon "Discouragement" 9.

29   Ibid.

30   Ralph Waldo Emerson, "The American Scholar," *American Heritage*, ed. Leon Howard, Louis B. Wright, and Carl Brode (Boston: D. C. Heath and Co., 1955), 1: 621.

31   Amy Carmichael, *Rose from Brier* (London: S.P.C.K., 1933), 175.

Chapter Three: Cut and Refocus

1   Winston S. Churchill, *Painting as a Pastime* (New York: Cornerstone Library, 1965), 7-8.

2   Churchill *Painting* 16.

3   Churchill *Painting* 31.

4   Margaret Millar, *Wall of Eyes* (reprint, New York: International Polygonics, Ltd., 1986), 176.

5   Anton Gill, *The Journey Back from Hell* (New York: William Morrow & Co., Inc., 1988), 456.

6   Peter Fabrizius (Max Knight and Joseph Fabry), *One and One Make Three* (Berkeley, Calif.: Benmir Books, 1988), 3-4.

7   Richard Nixon, *In the Arena* (New York: Simon & Schuster, 1990), 157-58.

Chapter Four: The Body and the Mind

1   Jeffrey M. Schwartz, M.D., and Sharon Begley, *The Mind & The Brain: Neuroplasticity and the Power of Mental Force* (New York: Harper Perennial, 2003), 250.

2   Dr. Michael Merzenich and Lennlee Keep, *The Brain Fitness Program* (Santa Fe Productions, Inc., 2007).

3   Michael Merzenich, M.D., quoted in Norman Doidge M.D., *The Brain That Changes Itself: Stories of Personal Triumph from*

the Frontiers of Brain Science (New York: Penguin Books, 2007), 55.

4 Schwartz and Begley *Mind* 320.

5 Schwartz and Begley *Mind* 366.

6 Schwartz and Begley *Mind* 375.

7 John Milton, *Paradise Lost*, Book I, lines 254-256. Source *An Oxford Anthology of English Poetry*, chosen and edited by Howard Foster Lowry and Willard Thorp with the assistance of Howard C. Horsford (New York: Oxford University Press, 1956), 354.

8 Paula Tallal quoted in Schwartz and Begley *Mind* 233.

9 Kenneth S. Wuest, *Philippians in the Greek New Testament* (Grand Rapids: William B. Eerdmans Publishing Co., 1942), 111.

10 Michael Merzenich, M.D., quoted in Doidge *Brain* 306.

11 Doidge *Brain* 307-08.

12 Doidge *Brain* 309.

13 Christine Larson, "Keeping Your Brain Fit," *U.S. News and World Report*, February 11, 2008, 49.

14 John J. Ratey, MD, with Eric Hagerman, *Spark: The Revolutionary New Science of Exercise and the Brain* (New York: Little, Brown and Company, 2008), 7.

15 Ratey *Spark* 243.

Chapter Five: Dream Blocks

1 Kenneth S. Wuest, *Romans in the Greek New Testament* (Grand Rapids: William B. Eerdmans Publishing Co., 1955), 209-11.

2 C. S. Lewis, *The Weight of Glory* (Grand Rapids: William B. Eerdmans Publishing Co., 1965), 15.

3 Søren Kierkegaard, *A Kierkegaard Anthology*, ed. Robert Bretall (Princeton, N.J.: Princeton University Press, 1946), 289, as quoted in Rollo May, *Man's Search for Himself* (New York: W. W. Norton, 1953), 101.

4 Lewis *Weight* 40-41.

5 Lewis *Weight* 9.

6 Lewis *Weight* 8-9.

7 Rollo May, *Man's Search for Himself* (New York: W. W. Norton, 1953), 100.

8 Socrates, quoted in May *Man's Search* 99.

9 Adolf Hitler, *Mein Kampf,* as quoted in William L. Shirer, *The Rise and Fall of the Third Reich* (New York: Simon & Schuster, 1959), 26.

10 Goethe quoted in Viktor E. Frankl et al., *Are You Nobody?* (Richmond: John Knox Press, 1973), 30.

11 Paul Tournier, *The Meaning of Persons* (New York: Harper & Row, 1957), 50.

12 Edward J. Boyer, "Consummate Entertainer Sammy Davis Jr. Dies at 64," *Los Angeles Times,* 17 March 1990, p. A28.

Chapter Six: Dream Builders

1 Viktor E. Frankl, *The Doctor and the Soul* (New York: Vintage, Random House, 1973), ix, xv.

2 Paul Tournier et al., *A Place for You* (New York: Harper & Row, 1968), 78-79.

3 Amy Carmichael, *Thou Givest – They Gather* (Fort Washington, PA: Christian Literature Crusade) 70-71.

4 Viktor E. Frankl et al., *Are You Nobody?* (Richmond: John Knox Press, 1973), 58.

5 Frankl *Are You Nobody?* 58.

6 Frankl *Are You Nobody?* 19.

7 Walter Trobisch, *The Complete Works of Walter Trobisch* (Downers Grove, Ill.: Inter-Varsity Press, 1987), 661.

8 C. S. Lewis, *Mere Christianity* (New York: Macmillan, 1964), 80-82.

9 C. S. Lewis, *Letters to an American Lady* (Grand Rapids: William B. Eerdmans Publishing Co., 1967), 41.

10 G. K. Chesterton, *St. Francis of Assisi* (London: Hodder & Stoughton), 110, as quoted in Tournier, *The Meaning of Persons* (New York: Harper & Row, 1957), 183.

Chapter Seven: Dream Bashers

1   George Matheson, "Make Me a Captive, Lord," originally called "Christian Freedom" in *Sacred Songs* (Row Dumbartonshire, Scotland, 1890). Source Robert Guy McCutcheon, *Our Hymnody: A Manual of the Methodist Hymnal,* with an index of scriptural texts, 2nd edition (New York: Abingdon Cokesbury Press, 1937), 384.

2   Norman Doidge M.D., *The Brain That Changes Itself: Stories of Personal Triumph from the Frontiers of Brain Science* (New York: Penguin Books, 2007), 209.

3   Rev. F. B. Meyer, *Christian Living* (Rahway, NJ: The Mershon Company), 88, 92-93.

4   C. S. Lewis, *Mere Christianity* (New York: Macmillan, 1964), 162.

Chapter Eight: Playing Cheetah

1   Amy Carmichael, *Kohila* (Fort Washington, Pa.: Christian Literature Crusade, n.d.), 139.

2   Winston S. Churchill, *Painting as a Pastime* (New York: Cornerstone Library, 1965), 7.

3   Churchill *Painting* 9-10.

4   Charles H. Spurgeon, source unknown.

Chapter Nine: Spirit Power

1   Charles H. Spurgeon, *Sermons of Rev. C. H. Spurgeon* (New York: Funk & Wagnalls, 1857), vol. 2, 366.

2   William Manchester, *American Caesar: Douglas MacArthur 1880-1964* (Boston: Little, Brown & Co., 1978), 702.

3   Alan Pifer and Lydia Bronte, eds., *Our Aging Society* (New York: W. W. Norton, 1986), 4, 11, 12.

4   Colin Turnbull, *The Human Cycle* (New York: Touchstone, Simon & Schuster, 1983), 229.

5   Turnbull *Human Cycle* 257-58.

6   C. H. M., *Notes on the Book of Numbers* (Chicago: Fleming H. Revell Company), 422, 425.

7   C. H. M. *Numbers* 423-24.

8   Peter Fabrizius (with Max Knight and Joseph Fabry), *One and One Make Three* (Berkeley, Calif.: Benmir Books, 1988), 131.

9   Salk Institute for Biological Studies, "Human Brains Do Sprout New Cells According to New Salk Study" (November 1, 1998), http://www.salk.edu/news/pressrelease_details. php?press_id=52.

10 Salk Institute for Biological Studies, "Salk researchers reprogram adult stem cells in their natural environment" (July 1, 2008), http://www.salk.edu/news/pressrelease_details. php?press_id=228.

11 John J. Ratey, M.D., *A User's Guide to the Brain: Perception, Attention, and the Four Theaters of the Brain* (New York: Vintage Books, 2002), 366.

12 Science Watch, "Salk's Fred H. Gage on Neurogenesis in the Adult Brain," (November/December 2005), http://archive. sciencewatch.com/nov-dec2005/sw_nov-dec2005_page3. htm.

13 Mary Carmichael, "Stronger, Faster, Smarter," *Newsweek*, March 26, 2007, 43.

14 Salk Institute for Biological Studies, "Exercise in a pill" (July 31, 2008), http://www.salk.edu/news/pressrelease_details. php?press_id=306.

15 Turnbull *Human Cycle* 226.

16 Rev. Robert Jamieson, D.D., Rev. A. R. Fausset, A.M., Rev. David Brown, D.D., *A Commentary Critical, Experimental and Practical on the Old and New Testaments* (Grand Rapids: William B. Eerdmans Publishing Co., 1945), vol. I., 194.

17 C. H. Spurgeon, *Metropolitan Tabernacle Pulpit*, vol. 39, 164-65.

18 Spurgeon *Sermons* 378.

Chapter Ten: Making Bad Times Good

1   Amy Carmichael, *Kohila* (Fort Washington, Pa.: Christian Literature Crusade, n.d.), 130.

2   Charles H. Spurgeon, *Sermons of Rev. C. H. Spurgeon* (New York: Funk & Wagnalls, 1857), vol. 2, 195.

3   Dr. Susan Vaughan quoted in Norman Doidge M.D., *The Brain That Changes Itself: Stories of Personal Triumph from the Frontiers of Brain Science* (New York: Penguin Books, 2007), 221.

4   C. S. Lewis, *Letters to an American Lady* (Grand Rapids: William B. Eerdmans Publishing Co., 1971), 110.

5   Rollo May, *Art of Counseling* (Nashville: Abingdon Press, 1967), 162.

Index

A

Adams, Jay
  depression and sin 38–39
  inaccuracy in his treatment of
    Freud 42
  on success of Dr. G. L.
    Harrington 40–41
adult stem cells
  plasticity of 215
aging. *See* neurogenesis
  accepting old age as a time of
    great meaning 200–201,
    201–202
  as time for sharing wisdom
    198–200
  as time to reflect on
    accomplishments 194
  as vital link in the continuity
    of life 211–213, 213–214
  importance of society
    embracing old age as a
    time of honor 208–210
  loss of productivity not
    inevitable 203–204
  on harm caused by negative
    expectations 197–198
  on hope posed by advances
    in brain research 214
  on the unique tasks of old
    age 204–206, 206–207,
    207–208
  opportunity for deeper
    worship 210–211
  proximity to death and
    eternity 219–221,
    222–226
  reaction to death of a parent
    218–219
  support for caregivers
    202–203
  value of confronting our fears
    of aging 226–227
  value of exercise 216–218
Alzheimer's Association
  recommended diet 101
amygdala
  role in emotions 94
Anger, Ambassador Per
  did not fit stereotype of aging
    204
Arnold, Matthew
  quotes from "Rugby Chapel"
    12, 15, 16
Attention Deficit Disorder
    (ADD)
  connection with use of
    electronic media 100–
    101

W

Elizabeth R. Skoglund is a licensed marriage, family therapist practicing in Glendale, California. Prior to starting a private practice, she was a secondary school teacher as well as a school counselor. She has published over 33 books as well as contributed articles to many publications. Her website is www.elizabethskoglund.com.

Also by Elizabeth Skoglund:

Found Faithful: The Timeless Stories of Charles Spurgeon, Amy Carmichael, C. S. Lewis, Ruth Bell Graham, and Others Who Triumphed over Pain

Gifts from the Hearth: Your Guide to Hospitality

Secrets of the Second Half: Living Well for the Rest of Your Life

Before I Die: A Practical Guide for End-of-Life Issues

Bright Days, Dark Nights; With Charles Spurgeon in Triumph Over Emotional Pain

A Quiet Courage: Per Anger, Wallenberg's Co-Liberator of Hungarian Jews

Amma: The Life and Words of Amy Carmichael of Dohnavur

Life On the Line

Safety Zones

Beyond Loneliness

To Anger, With Love

"Loneliness"

Contributor to *NIV Senior's Devotional Bible*

Contributor to the *Evangelical Dictionary of Theology*, Walter A. Elwell, Editor

Burnout (ebook)

www.ingramcontent.com/pod-product-compliance
Lightning Source LLC
Chambersburg PA
CBHW031151270326
41931CB00006B/226